WHEN
GRACE
WALKS
IN

Stacey Thacker

HARVEST HOUSE PUBLISHERS
EUGENE, OREGON

Cover by Connie Gabbert Design & Illustration

Cover photos © Komlev/Shutterstock

Published in association with Books & Such Management, 52 Mission Circle, Suite 122, PMB 170, Santa Rosa, CA 95409-5370, www.booksandsuch.com.

When Grace Walks In

Copyright © 2018 Stacey Thacker
Published by Harvest House Publishers
Eugene, Oregon 97408
www.harvesthousepublishers.com

ISBN 978-0-7369-7010-5 (pbk)
ISBN 978-0-7369-7011-2 (eBook)

Library of Congress Cataloging-in-Publication Data

Names: Thacker, Stacey, 1971- author.
Title: When grace walks in / Stacey Thacker.
Description: Eugene, Oregon : Harvest House Publishers, 2018.
Identifiers: LCCN 2018000560 (print) | LCCN 2018016523 (ebook) | ISBN 9780736970112 (ebook) | ISBN 9780736970105 (pbk.)
Subjects: LCSH: Bible. Ephesians—Criticism, interpretation, etc. | Grace (Theology) | Christian women—Religious life.
Classification: LCC BS2695.52 (ebook) | LCC BS2695.52 .T43 2018 (print) | DDC 227/.506—dc23
LC record available at https://lccn.loc.gov/2018000560

Printed in the United States of America

18 19 20 21 22 23 24 25 26 / VP-SK / 10 9 8 7 6 5 4 3 2 1

For Emma, Abigail,
Caroline, and Alison.
You are so loved.

Contents

Introduction 7

How to Use This Book 15

1. Worth 17

2. Grace-Made 35

3. Belong 51

4. Bow the Knee 67

5. Walk Worthy 97

6. In the Trenches 115

7. Three Ways Not to Lose Your First Love 141

Start a Girlfriend Group 161

The Word 163

LIFE Bible Study Method at a Glance 179

Notes 181

Introduction

(Please Don't Miss This)

Intense.

That's the word I would have chosen to describe the previous nine months of my life. Every square inch of that time had been filled with intensity. I was spread too thin. I had responsibilities as a wife and mother. My writing was in high gear. On top of that, my daughter's health was fragile. Burdened and busy, I was surviving, but just barely.

Then an opportunity to attend a Christian women's conference in Nashville with friends presented itself. Many of the speakers serving at the event were women I knew and loved to follow through their online ministries and books. But I was sure that, with life so crazy, I couldn't go. Cautiously, I discussed the potential weekend away with my husband. He said, "You know, I think we can make it work, and even more, I think you should go. You need this."

I nearly broke down in tears at his encouragement. I was downright ecstatic with anticipation a few weeks later when I walked off the plane in Nashville. God had pulled this off in the most amazing way, and I was ready to see what he had in store for me.

My friend Erin had organized our trip down to every iconic food stop we needed to enjoy while in town. Her first choice was a place called Hattie B's that served Nashville hot chicken. Sometime after I downed my ~~mildly~~ extremely hot portion and just after we took a group selfie in front of the establishment's sign, I felt myself beginning to relax. (It's entirely possible the hot chicken was also having its full effect.) Something loosened in my spirit, and I let go of the first layer of stress I had so tightly wound around my heart. I exhaled slowly, and simultaneously my phone beeped with a message from home.

My daughter had the flu.

I received several subsequent messages with details, and I understood this flu was likely to duplicate itself among my other family members, rapidly and relentlessly. Suddenly my weekend away felt extravagant. My family needed me in this crisis moment, and I was hundreds of miles away, not positioned to be of any help to them for several days.

My sweet friends gathered and prayed over the situation, and I called my husband, who by then also wasn't feeling well. Later that night, as I lay on the pull-out couch in my hotel room, I wondered why God would allow my family to be sick while I was in another state. My heart felt heavy with guilt over the unexpected turn of events.

The next morning my guilt mixed with a hint of bitterness. I needed this weekend away with friends, and now my heart was divided. I wasn't even sure I'd be able to absorb any of the workshop messages that morning, but I went anyway. Sipping on my giant cup of coffee, I slid into a seat for a session with Bible teacher Kelly Minter. I remember looking at her as she casually talked to several women before the session began. She had no idea what I was experiencing as I sat there swimming in emotions.

I thought, *This had better be good. I really hope she knows what she's talking about. I need to hear something that's going to make a real difference in my life.* I don't know if that was a prayer; I think it was more of a conversation with myself inside my head. Jesus, of course, was privy to my almost prayer. He knew my thoughts before I owned up to them. And he was not a bit surprised or shocked by the intensity of my discouragement.

I pulled out my conference notebook and started taking notes as

Kelly began to share from her heart. My pen stopped cold when she turned to the Bible story about Mary and Martha in the book of Luke. You see, I get a little bit worked up about this pair of sisters. As she started reading the account of Jesus being welcomed into their home, the hairs on the back of my neck rose. I knew what was coming. Once again God would use this story to call out my inner Martha and tell me he had his eyes on me and my skewed view: feeling responsible for all the things and all the people.

Martha and I have quite a bit in common. She is my people. We have a mutual understanding about how the world works and about how the world largely depends on us. I figured Jesus was going to draw my focus to that part of the story. Now I wasn't only bitter; I was annoyed.

As Kelly read through the passage, though, the Lord revealed a fresh truth my heart could not have needed more. Only it wasn't really about Martha in the kitchen, all worked up. Well, in part it was. But mostly my breath caught at what Jesus said to Martha about Mary.

> "Martha, Martha, you are worried and distracted by many things. One thing is necessary. Mary has chosen the better part. *It won't be taken away from her*" (Luke 10:41-42 CEB, emphasis mine).

In that moment the room disappeared, and as lovely as she was, I wasn't sitting and listening to Kelly Minter. Grace walked in, and I was sitting at the feet of Jesus. He was putting his hands on my shoulders and speaking directly to my soul: *Stacey, you are distracted by so many things. And all those things are going to pass away. Your family is going to get better. You are not home because I have set you apart this weekend to be here with me. And as you sit at my feet and listen to my Word, I will pour something into your heart that can't be taken away. Not ever.*

Tears pooled in my eyes at the sweetness of the Lord's gentle tending to my weary heart. He knew everything I had been carrying. And he absolutely knew my family was going to be okay. He also knew I needed the weekend because of what I had been going through for months and months. He could look down the road and know this time at his feet would be a deposit in my soul for the future, when my world would tilt and spin off its axis and my life would forever be changed. His Word that weekend prepared me for future, hidden things. And to think I almost missed it.

You probably picked up this book for at least one of several reasons. Maybe you've read a couple of my other books, or you really like the title or the pretty cover. Perhaps you picked it up in desperation, wanting to see if there was anything between the covers that would leap off the page. Maybe you said in your own heart something like I said at the conference: *I hope this girl knows what she's talking about, because who wants to read a boring book that ends up wasting my time?* It's totally okay if you're leaning more in that direction, because clearly you're my people too.

May I talk to you girlfriend to girlfriend right now? If we were sitting together at Panera, I would buy you dessert and your favorite drink, and then I would lean in to say this part because I want you to know I understand what you might be feeling. This is what I would say, dear friend:

When you draw near to Jesus and listen to the truth of his Word, he deposits something into the very core of who you are that can't be taken away. It's not a temporary fix or Band-Aid placed over a gaping wound. His Word, when it falls on soft hearts, changes us. It prepares us. It encourages us. Choosing to sit at his feet is never a waste of time. It is truly an encounter with grace.

This book is inspired by the book of Ephesians. Why this book now? I've asked myself that question. I almost put it aside for a while. Over the past few years, as I have walked with God, I've experienced almost unbearable suffering, death, grief, and illness. My family has had trials with work, finances, health, family, and in our daily lives. Every part of my life has experienced hardship, and it has tested me to the core.

I've thought long and hard about what I should be writing, especially considering what has happened in my life most recently, or even if I should be writing right now or taking a long break. But the bottom line is that I want to know Jesus and the power of his resurrection

Jesus is always
present with us.
I assure you he is.

personally. I don't want to miss what he wants to teach me simply because life has been hard. I also long to write words that point women to Jesus from the deepest parts of my life—even the broken parts. These experiences have wounded me, but I've found that time and again God brings healing, primarily through his Word. This journey has broken me in a way I hadn't expected.

There is sorrow and suffering—yes. But Jesus is always present with us. I assure you he is.

When I think about the Ephesians, I think of a group of people living in the middle of a hot and crazy culture who hated them because of their Savior. I think about a young preacher just trying to point them to Jesus. I think about a mentor named Paul, who had to tear himself away because God was calling him elsewhere. I think of more words written to their pastor than to anyone else in the Bible. I think of life-on-life ministry even when we can't be near.

I think of prayer. I think of overwhelming grace. I think of warfare my family has experienced and probably will undergo in the coming days. It makes me cry out, "Jesus, let me be a grace-made girl forever in you!" Finally, as I look forward, I want to love Jesus more and more. I don't want to stand on the other side of today's trials and hear, "What happened, girl? When did you lose your first love?" Do you?

I am choosing by faith to believe God has made a divine appointment for my heart here in the pages of Ephesians. I committed to writing this book over a year ago. I had no idea how much I would need it. God, of course, did. I also trust that he has a message for your heart, so I'm inviting you to come along with me. He wants to tell you that you are passionately pursued and incredibly loved. That changes everything about you. Dwell in that truth-filled grace for as long as you need to. I believe, as you do, that something will rise inside you, making it possible to walk out your faith differently. How do I know that? Because that same truth is changing my world even as I write these words.

I have come to believe there is a beautiful freedom in not only knowing who you are, but in knowing whose you are. You and I have been given the glorious gift of being God's girl. He wants to write his Word on our hearts.

Let's not miss it.
Let's lean in.
He won't take it away.

Looking forward,
Stacey

How to Use This Book

Please do me a favor: Read this book with your own Bible nearby. Maybe you have a beat-up 20-year-old Bible. Or maybe you recently purchased a journaling Bible, like me. I love those! Or perhaps you use your smartphone or computer when you study God's Word. Whatever works for you, have it with you as you read. Mark the verses we talk about, so you can easily find them later. Just remember to keep the "guide" in Girlfriends' Guide in mind. My greatest prayer is that when you're finished reading *this book*, you won't be able to wait to investigate in the Bible on your own.

At the beginning of each chapter, you'll find a list of key Scripture references. You might want to start by reading through them to prepare your heart for the words that follow.

You can, of course, read this book on your own and journal your way through it. I love doing that. But I've also put together a study guide for you at the end of each chapter. My hope is that you'll invite a few girlfriends to read through this book with you and let the guide do the work for you.

Another idea you might want to consider is starting a Girlfriend Group. What's different about a Girlfriend Group? I'm so glad you asked. This type of group is Word-driven and uses *When Grace Walks In* as a commentary to your conversation as you study the book of Ephesians. You can read more about Girlfriend Groups on pages 161-62. It can be as simple as taking the time to study the Scriptures, reading the book's chapters, showing up at your favorite coffee place, and answering the questions.

If you start any kind of group, be sure to let me know. And remember, I'm praying for you!

Worth

You are worth Jesus to God.

LOUIE GIGLIO[1]

Key Scriptures: Ephesians 1; Isaiah 44:1-22;
1 Corinthians 1:27-31; Hebrews 6:14

I was never cool.

One of the first indications was a hairstyle I was convinced would prove otherwise in middle school. Lured by the promise of looking just like one of Charlie's Angels, I asked my mom, my personal hair stylist, to cut my long hair. But I didn't want just any haircut. I wanted my hair to "feather" on the sides. Feathering was the definition of cool in the 1980s. I believed that if my hair was feathered, I would somehow magically transform into the cool girl at school. Copious amounts of Aqua Net hair spray might be involved, but the windswept look was worth it. You see, I wanted my hair to look just like my friend Julie's. Her glorious blond locks feathered back away from her face as if the wind had gently blown through and arranged them. Plus, her hair stayed that way all day. It was almost as if her hair decided on the first day of middle school to feather itself. I tried everything to look like her. It wasn't meant to be, I suppose. My hair had more of an awkward swoop with unfortunate curls compliments of an at-home permanent I also persuaded my mom to give me. She usually cooperated with my wishes. My hair did not.

It never did feather.

I fumbled my way through those years trying to be seen and trying to hide at the same time. Neither, like my hair, worked very well. Lately I've been thinking how my life now isn't so different from those days back in middle school. Maybe you can relate as well.

Insecurity

I was a smart kid and a hard worker in a bookish sort of way. Sadly, book smart did not necessarily translate into socially smart. I remember being pretty comfortable during class time, but it was a whole different story in the hallway. The bell would ring for us to move to a new class, and suddenly I was walking through my worst nightmare because boys and cool kids were everywhere. *I mean, can you feel yourself sweating?*

Today, my insecurity seems to rise as I try to measure up to the "cool kids." Only now it isn't the hallway between classes. It's on Instagram and in what all the other adorable women are posting online. While I try to hide the dark circles that have taken up permanent residence under my eyes and get my still-resistant hair to do anything remotely stylish, I hear whispers in my head that say, *Why are you even trying? You will never measure up.*

Fear

Insecurity may keep you from trying, but fear of failure could cause something else to happen. You might find yourself working twice as hard to make sure no one sees you are struggling. Just keep moving, and make sure no one knows what is really driving you. What is worse than failing? Failing in front of others.

Fear is a nasty taskmaster.

I had a coach during those same middle school years who was big on rules. They weren't bad in and of themselves, but for a girl like me who was a people pleaser, those rules became my haven. If I just did "it" all right, everything would be fine. She had a checklist I memorized and lived by:

- Weekly character development (check)

- Neat and tidy uniform (check)

- Good grades (all A's of course)

- Being a friend to all (check)

My fear of authority was strong and I certainly didn't want to end up on a list with "Shame" written at the top. I worked myself into a fit trying to avoid failure. Girls, can I tell you a secret? I still mentally check off those same types of things on Mondays while sipping my overcreamed coffee and trying to get my girls out the door to school. Only the coach has moved into my own heart. When your biggest fear is failure, you are driven to do all the things all the time. In the process, rest and peace get lost. My struggle is still real.

Undesirable

The hair feathering fiasco set me up nicely for more than a few years of wondering if I would ever be chosen.

> See, I know what it feels like to be passed by and ignored. My first memory of being passed by was in the eighth grade. I was one of the only girls not to have a date to our eighth grade dance. I really wanted one particular boy to ask me. But he chose someone else. I thought about staying home that night and watching a movie instead, but my mom encouraged me to pick out a pretty dress and go anyhow. She bought me a pink corsage, and I cried when she pinned it on me. [2]

Undesirable is a deeply felt emotion.

This feeling resurfaced this past year in the middle of my forties. I was reminded once again how easy it is to fade into the background of

your own life and play the wallflower. That same girl who felt undesirable in 1985 still pushes back feelings of being passed by or picked
last. Honestly, I felt both of those things within the last 24 hours. Who
wants a weary woman who looks tired, is busy raising four girls, and
can't quite keep her shopping list down to one trip per week?

Who wants that girl?

Jesus wants that girl. Then and now.

He whispers over my insecurities: *blameless.*

He persists in telling me when I fear failure: *free.*

He shouts over the voice that cries undesirable: *chosen.*

How do I know this for sure? Well, the Bible says, long ago, before
God laid the foundations of the world, he was thinking about you (and
me) and how much he loved us. In fact the book of Ephesians, chapter
3, verse 15 tells us that we were chosen and received our name from the
Father, from whom "all families in heaven above and on earth below
receive their names" (THE VOICE). He decided from the beginning of
time to adopt us as his daughters through his only Son, Jesus, and to
write his name over our hearts. Do you know how he felt about that?
He delighted in doing so. His plan was for us to be part of his special family. Being part of his family brings with it blessings of untold
worth, gifts we get to experience now and forever, and more importantly, access to our heavenly Father no one can hinder.

We all ask questions like, "Who am I?" and "What am I worth?"
Many of us seek the answer to these questions fervently. We might look
to the opinions of others for a clue. Maybe we read self-help books to
find answers, or we search social media for someone we want to be like
and imitate them. Too often we come away feeling as though we don't
measure up—mostly because we believe the lie we have to be enough in
the first place. It doesn't matter if you are a middle-school girl or somewhere in the middle of your life like me. Every one of us is searching.

> The answer to the question *Who am I?* isn't
> bound up in you at all; it's a treasure buried
> within the heart of your Father.

Knowing what God says about us will make a world of difference in how we view ourselves, as well as in how we live out our stories the way he planned from the beginning of time. But first we must shift our focus. This is no small thing. The answer to the question *Who am I?* isn't bound up in you at all; it's a treasure buried within the heart of your Father.

Jesus said during his earthly ministry, "I am the vine; you are the branches. Whoever abides in me and I in him, he it is that bears much fruit, for apart from me you can do nothing" (John 15:5). We grow from the vine. Our life is drawn from his. If we want to satisfy the longing of our hearts, we must go back to the source—the vine we are grafted into. But to abide in Christ and stay deeply connected to him, we must know and dwell in the truth of God's eternal Word. A.W. Tozer said, "The whole Bible and all the great saints of the past join to tell us the same thing...'Go back to the grass roots. Open your hearts and search the Scriptures.'"[3] That is exactly what we're going to do.

Searching Ephesians

Fortunately for us, from its beginning the book of Ephesians beckons us to mine this treasure by seeking God first. The apostle Paul wrote the letter of Ephesians. If you know a thing or two about him, you might know he was radically transformed from persecutor of the church to their pastor when he encountered the risen Christ on the road to Damascus. His redeemed writings make up a large portion of the New Testament (second only to Luke's words). He penned this letter from prison in about AD 60, which places it historically near the end of the book of Acts. It was written to his dear son in the faith, Timothy, whom he left in charge of the church in Ephesus.

The Bible contains more words written to Timothy than to any other person. Their correspondence records Paul's heart to equip his young disciple. Along the way, we have the blessing of watching this relationship unfold through the words we know as Ephesians and 1 and 2 Timothy.

Ephesus was a world-class city you might compare to New York or Paris today. It hummed with activity and people. A seaport town,

Ephesus was open to the religious influences of several cultures that arrived on her doorstep in abundance every day. The Ephesians worshiped most of the Greek and Roman gods, but especially the goddess Artemis. They built a massive temple in her honor, which is commonly listed as one of the Seven Wonders of the World. The people of Ephesus were enthusiastically and financially invested in every area of pagan religion.

Still, the young church of Christ thrived here even amid great evil and severe persecution. The church in Ephesus was made up of ordinary people like you and me. They were leaders, shopkeepers, fathers, mothers, and tradesmen. They were married, widowed, and single. Some of them were even slaves.

Scholars believe this letter traveled from province to province in Asia, and then finally landed and stayed in Ephesus. Paul had spent three years in Ephesus, his ministry having a profound impact on the city. He knew the church in Ephesus was strategically positioned. We learn from Acts 19 that the gospel spread from Ephesus to all of Asia, probably because the world came to her doorstep to trade. It's no wonder Paul wrote to this group of believers. He wanted them to know and remember the truth, and since he couldn't be with them, he put that truth down on paper. He also wrote passionately because he cared deeply for the believers in Ephesus.

Witness with me this emotional scene from the last few moments Paul spent with his beloved Ephesian friends. He had left Ephesus for Macedonia and returned on his way to Jerusalem by way of Miletus, and while in Miletus, he sent for the elders of the church from Ephesus to join him. Paul knew he would never see this group of believers again. And from the emotions displayed here, we know they knew it too. Luke, the author of the book Acts, described the scene:

> He knelt down and prayed with them all. And there was much weeping on the part of all; they embraced Paul and kissed him, being sorrowful most of all because of the word he had spoken, that they would not see his face again. And they accompanied him to the ship (Acts 20:36-38).

Does this grip your heart like it does mine? This group of men was saying a last good-bye with *weeping on the part of all*. Their hearts were broken with love for one another and the knowledge this was their final time face-to-face. If you have ever wept your way through the final scene of *The Lord of the Rings: The Return of the King*, you might understand this. Paul, like Frodo, had to leave his friends and his role in their everyday story behind. It was like turning to the last page of a truly good book. While their stories in Ephesus would keep going, his was coming to a bittersweet end.

This reminds me of how I feel about the women I've had the chance to minister to in the past year. I met Debora and Jen in a moms' summer Bible study group. They were going through the *Hope for the Weary Mom Devotional* I wrote, and I was invited to join them for one of their group times. We connected instantly, and the following year we saw one another frequently on Sunday mornings while dropping off our kids at Sunday school. Later, when I signed up to lead a small group through a Bible study called *Open Your Bible* at my church on Wednesday nights, they joined. We spent several weeks doing my absolute favorite thing—learning and loving the Word of God and encouraging one another.

A few weeks later, in the spring of 2017, my life took an abrupt turn. My husband was in the ICU for eleven days after he experienced a sudden cardiac arrest.* While he was recovering, Debora and Jen came to visit me. They brought me coffee, gift cards, and notes, and more importantly they encouraged me by just being present. When we were nearing the end of our time together, they asked to pray for my family. Of course, I said yes.

Debora, who is from Brazil, said, "Jen, maybe you should pray because my English isn't so good when I pray." I reached toward her and said, "Debora, I would love to hear you pray in Portuguese." She agreed, and both women prayed bold and sweet prayers over my family—one in Portuguese, and the other in English. We were all crying

---

* As I'm writing this book, the story of Mike's cardiac arrest and his healing is still being written. You may find it coming up from time to time in this book, but the entire story is not here. Thank you for your grace in letting our deeply personal story unfold in due time. I promise it will.

when we said amen. As they left, I thought about how I might have been the one ministering to them in the beginning, but they had certainly ministered to me in the process. This is what happens when we engage in life-on-life ministry—we minister to each other. I think this was what Paul and the church leaders of Ephesus felt as well.

> Relationships found in Christ and nurtured around
> the Word of God grow the deepest kind of bond.
> A bond we can't see or explain. And it never ends,
> because in Christ our relationship is forever.

Hold Nothing Back

> I have not held back from telling you the purpose of God
> in all its dimensions (Acts 20:27 THE VOICE).

Paul wasn't accustomed to holding anything back. The vigor with which he persecuted the church before his salvation became the passion with which he later ministered. Paul was all in, you might say. He worked side by side with the Ephesians, and he taught them the same things whether they were Jews or Greeks. He told them to turn to God and have faith in Christ Jesus. It was with equal passion that he wrote this first letter to Timothy and the church that had captured his heart. He takes a breath and exhales, and what comes out, in the original Greek, is one stunning, unbroken sentence. He holds nothing back this time either, saying,

> Blessed be the God and Father of our Lord Jesus Christ,
> who has blessed us in Christ with every spiritual blessing
> in the heavenly places, even as he chose us in him before
> the foundation of the world, that we should be holy and
> blameless before him. In love he predestined us for adop-
> tion to himself as sons through Jesus Christ, according to
> the purpose of his will, to the praise of his glorious grace,
> with which he has blessed us in the Beloved. In him we have

redemption through his blood, the forgiveness of our trespasses, according to the riches of his grace, which he lavished upon us, in all wisdom and insight making known to us the mystery of his will, according to his purpose, which he set forth in Christ as a plan for the fullness of time, to unite all things in him, things in heaven and things on earth.

In him we have obtained an inheritance, having been predestined according to the purpose of him who works all things according to the counsel of his will, so that we who were the first to hope in Christ might be to the praise of his glory. In him you also, when you heard the word of truth, the gospel of your salvation, and believed in him, were sealed with the promised Holy Spirit, who is the guarantee of our inheritance until we acquire possession of it, to the praise of his glory (Ephesians 1:3-14).

Can you read that in one breath? I wonder how many times Paul had to re-dip his pen in the ink to slide it across the page. He was probably moving so fast that each line wore thin to the edge. I imagine he might have had tears in his eyes as he considered what he most wanted his friends in Ephesus to know. He was eager for them to remember what he had taught them about the truth of the gospel. This was always Paul's heartbeat—the gospel story.

Milton Vincent wrote, "In most of Paul's letters to the churches, sizeable portions of them are given over to rehearsing gospel truths...Re-preaching the gospel and then showing how it applied to life was Paul's choice method for ministering to believers."[4] In his word-soaked, gospel-packed opening sentence, Paul was sure to pull the thread of salvation through each member of the Trinity—because each part is crucial. I love how this note I found in The Voice Bible translation explains it:

This letter begins with praise and thanksgiving to:

1. God the Father, who blesses us,

2. Jesus, who redeems us,

3. The Holy Spirit, who seals us.[5]

We get to soak it all in as well. I realize this might seem like a lot of doctrine for the opening lines of a letter. But we don't want to miss any of it; these things matter deeply. Let's dig in here together.

The Gospel: The Father, Who Blesses

Blessed be the God and Father of our Lord Jesus Christ, who has blessed us in Christ with every spiritual blessing in the heavenly places (Ephesians 1:3).

Please bear with me as we dive into the grammar of this text, because this is rich with meaning. I am a giddy word-girl over this part. If you are too, get your highlighter ready. Pull out those pens and mark this in your journaling Bible. Whatever you do, don't miss it!

The starting point is God. You are not the starting point. I'm certainly not either. God, the Father who has blessed us, is first. We bless him because he has blessed us.

The blessings are past tense. The word used for "blessed" in the Greek is in the aorist tense. This means, the action of blessing us has already happened. The writer is saying to take note—the blessings are already yours.

We are blessed in Christ. Everyone who comes to salvation through his redemptive work on the cross has access to every spiritual blessing in the heavens. Our blessings from the Father are completely based on the finished work of Christ. We don't earn them or deserve them. They are all because of his completed work on the cross. Do you see how at every point in the first few sentences of this letter that Paul is shifting our focus off of ourselves? Don't you find it freeing? Let's keep going. There is more to find, and I think it is worth it to work through more.

Paul uses an adjective to describe an attribute of God's character, a verb to describe how God acts, and a noun to describe what God gives us.

Blessed be the God and Father of our Lord Jesus. (Adjective)
Who *blesses* us. (Verb)

You are his daughter.
He has blessed you. It's
who he is. It's what he
does. It's what he gives.

With every spiritual *blessing.* (Noun)

This takes me back to Hebrews 6:14. The author, when reflecting on how God worked in Abraham's life, remembered this word from God: "I promise that I'll bless you with everything I have—bless and bless and bless!" (MSG). God holds nothing back in Christ. He gives us everything he has. He blesses and blesses and blesses.

Let me confess something to you. I like to think you like me because of what I do and who I am. I want to impress you. But when I look at the 25 words in Ephesians 1:3 (ESV), I'm reminded that my search for worth and significance begins and ends *here.*

Recently I was listening to a teaching by Elisabeth Elliot on this passage. She reminded me that as women, we long to be known. Maybe we want to live in such a way that others will see us and think we're extraordinary and special. But this is "our true significance. Blessed by the blessed Father with *every* blessing in Christ."[6] What more do we need? Oh, my friend, you are his daughter. He has blessed you. It's who he is. It's what he does. It's what he gives.

The Gospel: The Redeemer, Who Redeems

In him we have redemption through his blood, the forgiveness of our trespasses, according to the riches of his grace (Ephesians 1:7).

Keep reading in the first chapter of Ephesians, and you will see that plan unfold. The gospel story moves on, and we see God is a redeemer. He rescues. He recovers. He has done so from the beginning.

During a time of difficulty last spring, God planted me firmly in the pages of Isaiah. Guess who I found there.

- Now, hear, O Jacob my servant, Israel whom I have *chosen*! Thus says the LORD who made you, who formed you from the womb and will help you. Fear not, O Jacob my servant, Jeshurun whom I have *chosen* (Isaiah 44:1-2, emphasis mine).

- Thus says the LORD, the King of Israel and his *Redeemer*, the LORD of hosts: "I am the first and I am the last; besides me there is no god" (Isaiah 44:6, emphasis mine).

- Remember these things, O Jacob, and Israel, for you are
  my servant; I *formed* you; you are my servant; O Israel, you
  will not be forgotten by me. I have blotted out your transgressions like a cloud and your sin like mist; return to me,
  for I have *redeemed* you (Isaiah 44:21-22, emphasis mine).

I found the heart of our redeemer crying out for his children, calling them home, once again wooing them back to himself. This is God's
covenant promise to his family: *I will help you, whom I have chosen. I
will not forget you.* The beauty of the gospel story is that now in Christ
we are part of that family too. This has always been God's plan.

Close your eyes and listen to the heart of your redeemer. Can you
hear the same echo of God's through Paul from the words of Isaiah?
"The gospel so beautifully reminds us Jesus is mindful of us and has
been forever."[7] He will not forget us. He has chosen us and redeemed
us. He forgives all our transgressions, and they disappear as though a
vapor in Christ.

Israel's redeemer and the Ephesians' redeemer are one. These pas-
sages tell the same story. God chose us in him before the world was
formed. He purposed for us to be holy and blameless. He adopted us
into his covenant family. He made this possible through Christ. He
not only chose us, but he planned it beforehand. We weren't an afterthought. To me, there is such a sweetness here.

Do you ever feel left out and alone? Does it seem like the world has
passed you by? You can be assured that your redeemer has not. Maybe
you feel not only left out, but weak and small. This is not a problem
for Jesus. He purposely seeks out the common. I love the reassurance
Paul gave to his friends in Corinth on this same topic. (The letter to
the church in Corinth was written while Paul was in Ephesus. Paul
often wrote similar words to different groups of people. I think that
was because these were not only his personal soapbox issues; they were
everyone else's too. I know they are for me).

Paul wrote,

> But celebrate this: God selected the world's foolish to bring
> shame upon those who think they are wise; likewise, He

selected the world's weak to bring disgrace upon those who think they are strong. God selected the common and the castoff, whatever lacks status, so He could invalidate the claims of those who think those things are significant. So it makes no sense for any person to boast in God's presence. Instead, credit God with your new situation: you are united with Jesus the Anointed. He is God's wisdom for us and more. He is our righteousness and holiness and redemption. As the Scripture says: "If someone wants to boast, he should boast in the Lord" (1 Corinthians 1:27-31 THE VOICE).

Here as well as in Ephesians chapter 1, all the credit goes to God, who has redeemed us in Christ. He is our *righteousness and holiness and redemption*. God knew what he was doing when he chose the weak, foolish, and insignificant in this world. The world may view us as nothing more than common and as castoffs, but when God sees us, he sees Christ. This is a beautiful and freeing truth. We do nothing here. We simply boast in him "to the praise of his glory" (Ephesians 1:12).

The Gospel: The Holy Spirit, Who Sealed You

Every blessing we receive from God is released by the sacrifice of Christ. They are all ours forever. But it gets even better.

> In him you also, when you heard the word of truth, the gospel of your salvation, and believed in him, were sealed with the promised Holy Spirit, who is the guarantee of our inheritance until we acquire possession of it, to the praise of his glory (Ephesians 1:13-14).

The moment you heard the word of truth and you claimed your salvation by faith, you were secured and sealed with the promised Holy Spirit. This seal "confirms and authenticates your faith, placing beyond a doubt you belong to God."[8] His mystery now revealed, you are his and always will be. He has set you apart and hidden you in Christ, safe in the shelter of his wings, protected from the Enemy, who would like to convince you otherwise.

The Holy Spirit also serves as a down payment of even greater blessings that await us in heaven. What is coming is even greater than what we have now. But we do have something now—we have the promise. As Tony Merida wrote, "God is not just telling us about something in the future, He is bringing the future into the present so that we may taste what the future is like."[9] Now we are spiritually in a place of victory in Christ in the heavenly places and blessed with every spiritual blessing. Someday we'll join him there physically. What we were made for will be understood and enjoyed to the full extent of God's divine purpose. And you better believe we will worship.

Why Wait? Worship Now

Alexander Maclaren said,

> *God blesses us by gifts; we bless Him by words.* The aim of His act of blessing is to evoke in our hearts the love that praises. We receive first, and then, moved by His mercies, we give. Our highest response to His most precious gifts is that we shall "take the cup of salvation, and call upon the name of the Lord," and in the depth of thankful and recipient hearts shall say, "Blessed be, God who hath blessed us."[10]

His purpose in blessing us is to draw out our hearts in praise to him. These good and perfect gifts are the foundation of who we are and the only measure of our worth that matters. When we preach the gospel to our own hearts, we are wonderfully reminded that Christ wins every time and in everything. And because we are in him, we do too.

How do our hearts hold the blessings? They cannot contain them. We receive them, give thanks, and bless his holy name. It's the very name he has beautifully written on our hearts.

> God chose us to be in a relationship with Him even before He laid out plans for this world; He wanted us to live holy lives characterized by love, free from sin, and blameless before Him (Ephesians 1:4 THE VOICE).

God says our names in Christ are:
   Chosen.
   Loved.
   Free.
   Blameless.
Who wants that girl?
Jesus wants that girl. And he died to make it true.

On the days my heart is ready to receive it, I don't hide in the middle of my life and play a wallflower. I dance in the kitchen while washing dishes, even though my hair still isn't close to feathering.

BIBLE STUDY

Encouragement

Ephesians 1:3-14

Connection

1. Share one statement from the chapter that was most significant to you and why.

2. In what other ways have you been tempted to draw your worth from the world instead of the Word?

3. Has anyone made an impact on your walk with the Lord in the same way Paul did for the Ephesians? What was it about them that made them so special?

Growth

1. Write and reflect on how your holiness is made possible.

2. Memorize Ephesians 1:3 (ESV): Blessed be the God and Father of our Lord Jesus Christ, who has blessed us in Christ with every spiritual blessing in heavenly places.

My Notes:

_____

_____

_____

_____

_____

Grace-Made

We need the gospel every day.

Tony Merida[1]

Key Scriptures: Ephesians 2:1-10;
Ephesians 3:1-13; John 8:1-11; 1 Timothy 1:15

She was as good as dead. Perhaps it would be better that way. Only minutes before she had been wrenched from the darkness and tossed into the street—discarded and accused. They were circling now, the vultures who had passed judgment on her so quickly she couldn't see straight.

Not that she was innocent. She wasn't, of course. Caught in the act, she was as guilty as they said she was. And they weren't mincing words. Yet they seemed to have a purpose greater than merely her condemnation. They wanted to use her as some sort of object lesson. Oh, she had been used before—this was not altogether unfamiliar territory. She always failed, but perhaps the teacher they sought would not. Did it really matter, though? Her fate was sealed; they'd already chosen their stones to throw.

But instead of pelting her, they turned their accusatory words like stones toward him. Standing her before him with a declaration of the Law she had broken, they waited for him to say something. Anything. The crowd waited. She waited.

He said nothing. Instead Jesus bent down and pressed his finger into the dirt—the dirt he created—and began to write. Perhaps it was for the crowd gathered to hear him teach or for the broken-down, shame-covered girl in front of him. Or it was directed to the scribes and Pharisees waiting to trap him with a single word. We don't know. And then Jesus stood and said, "Let him who is without sin among you be the first to throw a stone at her" (John 8:5).

He didn't say another word to them. He went back to writing in the dirt. Instead of judging her obvious sin, he judged their hidden sins. With their consciences seared by his question, one by one they dropped their stones to the ground. The judges walked away, shaking their heads in disbelief.

Ironically, the only one truly able to throw a stone at her tossed a simple question instead: "Woman, where are they? Has no one condemned you?" (verse 8). Seeing they had all gone, her own belief rising to meet the forgiveness extended to her, she answered, "'No one, Lord.' And Jesus said, 'Neither do I condemn you; go, and from now on sin no more'" (verse 11).

> Once marked for destruction, she was now marked with grace and mercy.

Jesus did for her what she could not have done for herself. He forgave her and simultaneously rescued her. Warren Wiersbe wrote, "For Jesus to forgive this woman meant that He had to one day die for her sins. Forgiveness is free, but it is not cheap."[2] Not only did he not cast a stone; he willingly took her punishment and marched straight to the cross with it. Once marked for destruction, she was now marked with grace and mercy.

When Grace Walks into Your Story

Grace walked into the story of the woman caught in adultery. She was dead—or at least she deserved death for her sin. She expected it. But the gospel of grace she found in Jesus was better than she could have imagined.

Paul knew this grace-giver too—the grace-giver who stepped into his story as well. Paul was more of the stone-thrower type of sinner himself—his need for grace was just as great. One day he came face-to-face with the same Jesus the adulterous woman met. Paul never got over it:

> I became a servant and preacher of this gospel by the gift of God's grace as He exercised His amazing power over me. I cannot think of anyone more unworthy to this cause than I, the least of the least of the saints. But here I am, a grace-made man, privileged to be an echo of His voice and a preacher to all the nations of the riches of the Anointed One, riches that no one ever imagined (Ephesians 3:7-8 THE VOICE).

In encountering Jesus, Paul encountered grace. Radically remade, he was rerouted. God's amazing power overwhelmed Paul with riches he never knew existed. He later wrote to Timothy, declaring, "Here's a statement worthy of trust: Jesus the Anointed, the Liberating King, came into the world to save sinners, and I am the worst of them all" (1 Timothy 1:15 THE VOICE). God's grace was the reason Paul's life had been completely transformed. He had no doubt. "Paul's life reminds us that God can radically change anyone. Here we have a man who might formerly have been compared to a terrorist now writing the New Testament."[3] Grace was Paul's story. When he saw himself, he saw God's merciful kindness and holy influence, turning him to Christ, strengthening his faith, and kindling his passion to serve God and preach to the nations the same riches over and over.

Paul declared this when he said, "I do not account my life of any value nor as precious to myself, if only I may finish my course and the ministry that I received from the Lord Jesus, to testify to the gospel of the grace of God" (Acts 20:24). He not only never got over the grace he'd been given; he never stopped talking about it. Every word was bathed in grace. Consider this:

> The epistles of Paul, only about one twelfth the size of the Old Testament and one-half the size of the four Gospels, employs the word *grace* and its derivatives no less than 144 times, *more often than all the rest of the Bible together and nearly twice as often as the whole Old Testament and the four Gospels together!* And then, in Paul's epistles the word *grace* is nearly always used doctrinally, in connection with *the dispensation of Grace.*[4]

He preached grace. He spoke of grace face-to-face with everyone. He wrote about grace, and every letter he sent opened and closed with grace. He truly was a grace-made man. He wanted to be sure the Ephesians saw grace at work in every facet of their story as well, so he told them the truth, without sugarcoating it one bit.

The truth Paul wanted to establish for the Ephesians was unforgettable: "And you were dead…" (Ephesians 2:1).

Any questions? A bit harsh? Paul didn't think so. Before he could talk about grace, he needed to get every bit of their junk out in the open. But before you feel too bad for them, you might want to notice that their junk is our junk too. Take a close look at the rest of verse 1 and verses 2 and 3:

> And *you were dead* in the trespasses and sins in which *you once walked*, following the course of this world, following the prince of the power of the air, the spirit that is now at work in the sons of disobedience—*among whom we all once lived* in the passions of *our flesh*, carrying out the desires of the body and the mind, and were by nature children of wrath, like the rest of mankind [emphasis added].

Paul isn't merely talking to the Ephesians; he's preaching to himself as well. If we believe the Word of God is for us, he is most definitely including us too. Paul wanted to shoot straight from the beginning.

"You can't be a little dead or a tiny bit sinful," he was saying. You were dead. Period.

Does this make you uncomfortable? I don't like to think about my life in the past too much. I would rather tell you all the things God is doing in my life now. We like a "therefore" much more than a "before." And, of course, the world doesn't like us to dwell on what we were before too much either. The whole "You were dead" doesn't play too well on social media. If you believe some of what you read there, you'll think you're good enough, smart enough, thin enough—simply just enough.

Tony Merida wrote,

> Now this is the complete opposite of what the world tells us about ourselves as humans. The world tells us that we are basically good, and if we just believe in ourselves, then we can do anything. While a spiritually dead person may indeed do amazing things because she is an image bearer of God—make works of art, play sports exceptionally well, make money, do humanitarian work—she can do nothing spiritually because she is not connected to the Vine.[5]

Keep in mind that Paul was good and righteous in the ways of the world. He was successful and smart, and he did his work exceptionally well. But he includes himself as one of the previously walking dead. We all are.

Paul adds more color to the story. We might as well just cringe right along with the Ephesians, because this is our truth too. Paul reminds them of their disobedient hearts that followed hard after the prince of the world. Make no mistake, they were "darkened in their understanding, alienated from the life of God because of the ignorance that is in them, due to their hardness of heart" (Ephesians 4:18).

Theologically, Paul is describing the doctrine of "total depravity," that is, all aspects of our being infected with the deadly disease of sin. Paul is also describing our "total inability: that is, morally we are not capable of responding to God apart from grace. The fact is we do not want to respond to God. But oh, how we need God's grace!"[6]

I'm praying like crazy I didn't just lose you, here in the beginning. Keep reading, but don't miss this fact: Every part of our hearts and lives has been sickened by sin. We don't have the ability to respond to God's grace without—you guessed it—his grace. In our disobedient, darkened, cut-off-from-God, self-focused lives, we don't even want grace. I know this isn't fun or easy to consider, but think back to the woman caught in adultery. She was dead. No hope. Cut off. She didn't even know to ask for grace. She just waited for the destruction she knew she deserved.

But grace walked in instead.

The Story

Have you ever walked out of a movie feeling cheated by the ending? Did you wait for the credits to roll, hoping there would be more footage or the hint of a sequel? We don't like to leave the story in a place that feels dark or unfinished. Recently, I read a gripping novel that ended with the main character dying on the final page. "This can't be the end!" I cried. Real tears pooled in my eyes…before I turned the page and saw a sneak peek at the next book in the series. Suddenly, hope welled within me. Of course, this also led me to buy the next book. Lucky for me, the author found a way to pitch the story truthfully in a new direction. Her solution was a thrilling rescue.

Paul understood the value of a thrilling rescue. He didn't leave the Ephesians dead and wandering about in the darkness, just as Jesus didn't. Paul contrasted their corrupt condition with the character of Christ. I imagine the Ephesians were sitting on the edge of their seats, just like I was when I realized there was a sequel to that book. They knew this story, and they knew it wasn't the end. They knew the "But God…" part was coming. And their hearts were encouraged to recall that very moment by one who had his own moment as well:

> God, being rich in mercy, because of the great love with which he loved us, even when we were dead in our trespasses, made us alive together with Christ—by grace you have been saved—and raised us up with him and seated us with him in the heavenly places in Christ Jesus, so that in

the coming ages he might show the immeasurable riches
of his grace in kindness toward us in Christ Jesus. For by
grace you have been saved through faith. And this is not
your own doing; it is the gift of God, not a result of works,
so that no one may boast (Ephesians 2:4-9).

Our deadness did not faze God. He saw our sin and responded in
love with great mercy. His heart was drawn to us with a desire to help
us in our miserable and afflicted state.

This should not surprise us at all. Jesus came to show us the heart of
God toward his people, and he said in Matthew 9:13, "'I am not here
to attend to people who are already right with God; I am here to attend
to sinners. In the book of Hosea, we read, "It is not sacrifice I want, but
mercy." Go and meditate on that for a while—maybe you'll come to
understand it'" (THE VOICE). Jesus is quoting Hosea 6:6 to some teachers of the Law who had a problem with him dining with sinners and tax
collectors. He was saying God's loyal and merciful love—his mercy—
ministers to sinners.

Where would we be without it? We would be dead. Instead, through
Jesus's life, death, and resurrection, God has made us alive with Christ.
He has also placed us in Christ, raised us up with him, and seated us
together with him in the heavenly places. We are no longer dead. We
are rescued and seated in the safest place possible. This positional truth
should change our lives forever. It is all Jesus, all by grace.

If Our Story Had a Theme Song

I grew up singing classic hymns in a little Baptist church in a small
town. The words to many hymns are written on my heart, though
sometimes you need to give me the tune and the first line. Nothing
takes me back to wooden pews and stain-glassed windows more than a
good hymn. I would venture to say that even if you've been to church
only once in your life, you're familiar with the song I can't stop singing as I write. Even if you prefer contemporary worship songs led by
a band, your worship team still on occasion probably breaks out this
one for an acoustic set:

> Amazing grace! (how sweet the sound)
>   That sav'd a wretch like me!
> I once was lost, but now am found,
>   Was blind, but now I see.
>
> 'Twas grace that taught my heart to fear,
>   And grace my fears reliev'd;
> How precious did that grace appear
>   The hour I first believ'd.

You know the hymn, but do you know the author was the wretch in the first verse? John Newton was a pastor and a hymn writer who lived from 1725–1807. He answered the call to ministry on his thirty-third birthday and served for 43 years, first in the village of Olney, then in the city of London. But prior to becoming a pastor, John Newton played the role of the rogue and wretch thoroughly. In his book on Newton's life, Tony Reinke wrote,

> He's mostly remembered for his hymn "Amazing Grace," for his radical spiritual transformation from a near-death shipwreck and for his work with William Wilberforce (1759–1833) to end the 'inhuman traffick' of the British slave trade, a trade in which he once sought his personal wealth and fortune.[7]

Wretched. Blind. A sinner. Fearful. A slave trader. Mortal. John Newton cried out for mercy on a storm-raging sea, and grace broke through and saved him—both physically and spiritually.

> By grace you have been saved through faith. And this is not your own doing; it is the gift of God, not a result of works, so that no one may boast (Ephesians 2:8-9).

John Newton did not save himself. He knew he wasn't worthy of grace. He understood God's grace to be a gift, which he humbly received. Much like Paul, he was forever changed when grace walked into his story. He saw this grace completely bound up in the person of Jesus Christ—one could not be received without the other. Jesus is our grace. And grace is Jesus.

Go ahead, slip "Jesus" into the hymn every time you sing *grace*. Do you see what once blind John Newton saw in amazing Jesus? He saw grace. There was absolutely no room for boasting within the verses penned here. This song was an autobiography of his redemption. And truthfully, it's ours too.

He said this in one of his sermons:

> The great God is pleased to manifest himself in Christ, as the God of grace. This grace is manifold, pardoning, converting, restoring, persevering grace, bestowed upon the miserable and worthless. Grace finds the sinner in a hopeless, helpless state, sitting in darkness, and in the shadow of death. Grace pardons the guilt, cleanses the pollution, and subdues the power of sin. Grace sustains the broken read, binds up the broken heart, and cherishes the smoking flax into a flame. Grace restores the souls when wandering, revives it when fainting, heals it when wounded, upholds it when ready to fall, teaches it to fight, goes before it in battle, and at last makes it more than conqueror over all opposition, and then bestows a crown of everlasting life. But all this grace is established and displayed by covenant in the man Christ Jesus, and without respect to him as living, dying, rising, reigning, and interceding in the behalf of sinners, would never be known.[8]

It pleased God to establish and display his grace in the person of Jesus. We would not know grace otherwise. John Newton and the apostle Paul could sing in unison, adding these words, "The saying is trustworthy and deserving of full acceptance, that Christ Jesus came into the world to save sinners, of whom I am the foremost" (1 Timothy 1:15). We might as well join their duet, because if Jesus saves wretches, we get to sing too.

The Epilogue (but not really)

It's good for us to remember how we used to be. When we look back we can see the hand of God writing out his story for our lives:

We remember that

- we used to just exist.

- we were lost and wandering.

- we were just like the world—owned by the prince of the air.

- we filled our minds with the passion for the world.

- we indulged our flesh and mind and did whatever we wanted.

- we were dead, living among the dead.

But like a light bursting into the darkness, God, with laser-focused intention, broke into our dead, dark world. And now we are alive and we

- see grace pursuing us, saving us, and repositioning us to be seated in a place of victory with our Liberating King for all eternity.

- stand as a living testimony to his unending, incredible, unfathomable grace and kindness—freely given.

- know we did not earn it—dead men earn only more death and destruction.

> It's powerful to remind someone of what God has wrought in their lives. It's also important to cast a vision in their hearts, letting them know a grand purpose is at work, and it's all for God's glory.

I'm struck by the contrast: Dead now alive. Wandering aimlessly and now walking in victory. Set for destruction and now marked with grace and mercy. Paul knew both sides of this transformation. He saw them before and after. It's powerful to remind someone of what God has wrought in their lives. It's also important to cast a vision in their hearts, letting them know a grand purpose is at work, and it's for God's glory:

> We are the product of His hand, heaven's poetry etched on lives, created in the Anointed, Jesus, to accomplish the good works God arranged long ago (Ephesians 2:10 THE VOICE).

Grace on the Move

My friend Britt understands heaven's poetry etched on lives and what it looks like to live out the works God has prepared for us to do. She has the sweetest business called *Gently Bound*, painting journal and Bible covers, personalizing them for her clients. Her works of art are placed in the hands of people who will open God's Word time and time again and remember grace walks into their stories too. Britt knows this from experience. She didn't always paint Bibles. At one time she didn't even own one.

About ten years ago, Britt realized, probably for the first time, that her life was a mess. Her father was a drug addict and her mother was involved with a man who was an alcoholic. Britt lived with her grandparents. They did the best they could, but by Britt's own description, "They were a little crazy." It didn't help matters that they lived in a rough part of Cincinnati, living on a meager Social Security income, and Britt was fighting a debilitating chronic illness that left her bedridden for days at a time. Her world came to a crashing halt when her brother was killed by local police and their story made national news. Britt fell into a deep depression. It was just too much.

What she didn't know was that grace was on the move in her life even as she was despairing. Her best friend at the time had become a Christian at a local church camp and invited Britt to come to youth group during her tenth-grade year of high school. This friend had loved Britt so well during the hardest days of her life, she was willing to say, "Yes. Of course I'll come with you."

That first night at a church she didn't know existed the week before, Britt made a deal with a youth leader. "I'll come to every church service you have for a month, and if I find this faith is worth my life, I'll accept

Jesus as my Savior." She made good on her word, attending every Bible study and service she could make it to—even one filled with 60-year-old women. She soaked up truth like a sponge, and at the end of the month, when that same youth leader remembered their deal, he asked her, "Britt, is it worth it? Do you want to know Jesus?"

She said yes.

Britt's life changed radically. She broke off every friendship she thought would hold her back from her newfound faith. She went to church camp, and she surrendered her life to serve Jesus in full-time ministry. She says, "I've seen since then the absolute sovereignty of God and how he has used my story to help other girls I meet today who are living hard stories too." Not only does Britt paint Bibles, but she uses her winsome way to reach out to college girls and share the love of Christ with them. Britt is walking in his ways—because grace walked into her story and changed her life forever.[9]

God's grace continues to move our story toward God. Someday we will see the completion of this work, when we're not only spiritually seated in Christ, but physically in his presence. For now, he has picked up his holy pen and written "Alive in Christ" across our lives. Paul is encouraging the Ephesians to let their lives speak from this place of awe. This is a calling for us as well. We are to allow heaven's poetry, God's story of grace, to leap off the pages of our hearts and point to him. Paul was confident of the good works God had arranged for him long ago. They landed him in prison, but he was not without hope:

> I cannot think of anyone more unworthy to this cause than I, the least of the least of the saints. But here I am, a grace-made man, privileged to be an echo of His voice and a preacher to all the nations of the riches of the Anointed One, riches that no one ever imagined. I am privileged to enlighten all of Adam's descendants to the mystery concealed from previous ages by God, the Creator of all, through Jesus the Anointed. Here's His objective: through the church, He intends now to make known His infinite and boundless wisdom to all rulers and authorities in heavenly realms. This has been His plan from the beginning,

one that He has now accomplished through the Anointed One, Jesus our Lord. His faithfulness to God has made it possible for us to have the courage we need and the ability to approach the Father confidently. So I ask you not to become discouraged because I am jailed for speaking out on your behalf. In fact, my suffering is something that brings you glory (Ephesians 3:8-13 THE VOICE).

Grace made Paul a preacher to the nations. Specifically, his special mission was to minister to the Gentiles who previously had been outcasts and aliens to God's people. This ministry was hidden, though planned from the beginning, until God revealed it in Christ. God's objective was the church—and Paul was honored to build it. He might have been a prisoner, but with the gospel framing his entire life, Paul was not discouraged. He implored the Ephesians not to be either. "The Good news about my trials is that God is forcing them to bow to His Gospel purpose and do good unto me by improving my character and making me more conformed to the image of Christ."[10] The gospel gives us the courage we need even in times of suffering. Our invitation is to approach the Father confidently. In Christ we have access and boldness to come and receive exactly what we need—grace and mercy—exactly when we need it (Hebrews 4:16).

When the Story Sticks with You

Grace levels the ground we stand on. It redeems prostitutes. It rescues murderers. And it places them side by side with girls like me, who have bought into the lie that they can work their way into God's story simply by being good. Grace is noble, and grace is radical.

And if I'm honest, I must admit a part of me is screaming, "That's not fair!" Are you shocked by this? Possibly feeling a little or a lot undone yourself? Oh, girl, I get it—I really do. Grace shoots a hole into *good enough* that is the shape of the cross and nothing less. Being grace-made is not pretty. It doesn't matter if you're a woman caught in adultery or one holding a stone in her hand. Grace involves the death of our rescuer, and because we are placed in him, we die too—to our sin and all our striving. The hope we have is this: Death isn't the end, but the beginning.

Grace stoops down. Jesus is jotting something in the soil of our hearts and looking at us with kind eyes, saying right to our souls, "Daughter, where are your good works? What are they worth? Do you have accusers too?"

We look around and say, "There is nothing and no one, Lord." Humbled and needy, we hear him say, "Well, I do not condemn you either; all I ask is that you go and from now on avoid the sins that plague you" (John 8:11 THE VOICE).

And only by his holy, other, unsettling grace, we will.

Grace shoots a hole
into *good enough* that
is the shape of the cross
and nothing less.

BIBLE STUDY

Encouragement

Ephesians 2:1-10

Connection

1. Share one statement from the chapter that was most significant to you and why.

2. With whom do you identify—the woman caught in public sin or the religious leaders covering up their hidden sins?

3. When did grace step into your story?

Growth

1. Write and reflect on your grace-made story. Share it with at least one person.

2. Memorize Ephesians 2:10 (THE VOICE): We are the product of His hand, heaven's poetry etched on lives, created in the Anointed, Jesus, to accomplish the good works God arranged long ago.

My Notes:

_____

_____

_____

_____

Belong

We must tie our identities to our unchanging, unflinching,
unyielding, undeniably good, and unquestionably loving God.

Lysa TerKeurst[1]

Key Scriptures: Ephesians 2:11-21; Ephesians
4:4-14; Isaiah 49:16; John 10:27-29

It probably won't surprise you after reading about my tragic middle school hair drama in chapter 1 that my epic lack of coolness only grew as I entered high school. I seemed to be left off the invitation list to pretty much every Saturday-night party. By that time, I understood why I wasn't invited, and it was probably a good thing. Still, the whispers and excuses I encountered on Monday morning didn't help my heart feel any better. I felt worse.

This continued until I went to Indiana University in the fall of 1989 and met my friend Robin. She was part of a Bible study I joined a few weeks after arriving. I think Robin must have sensed my lack of coolness and identified with me, because she told hilarious stories about growing up and high school, and about how she wasn't cool either. It was as if she was saying, *You belong here.* We bonded immediately. But

something else happened when I joined her Bible study. More important than discovering a kindred heart in Robin, whose friendship I still
cherish decades later, I uncovered the heart of my heavenly Father for
me. He spoke words that landed even deeper, and his whisper undid
every other rejection that had scarred my uninvited, uncool heart. He
said, *You belong to me.* And suddenly, I was home.

You Belong to Jesus

We've already talked about grace walking into our individual stories.
But it's just as beautiful to pull back and take a broader view of God's
story. Contemplating its vastness always touches my heart, filling me
with awe and wonder. I read his Word, and on page after page I see his
passionate pursuit of your heart and mine.

A few years ago, I read the Bible cover to cover in a little less than
90 days. I read for about an hour each day (with a couple of grace days
worked in) and completed all 66 books. I started on Memorial Day
and finished around Labor Day. I was—and still am—so grateful for
this journey through God's Word. From Genesis 1:1, "In the beginning,"
to the last words, which read "The grace of the Lord Jesus be with all.
Amen" (Revelation 22:21), I was radically moved. Somewhere in the
middle of that summer, the Bible became more than simply a book to
me. I'd always known it to be good, but the tremendous story of God's
grace pierced my heart and gave me a fresh glimpse of my redeemer.

God's heart has always been bent toward his people. The same God
who whispered to my heart my freshman year of college had been
doing it from the beginning of time. After 30 days of reading, I found
there is no one like our Lord:

> There is no one like you, Lord, and there is no God but
> you.... And who is like your people Israel—the one nation
> on earth whose God went out to redeem a people for him-
> self, and to make a name for yourself, and to perform great
> and awesome wonders by driving out nations from before
> your people, whom you redeemed from Egypt? You made
> your people Israel your very own forever, and you, Lord,
> have become their God (1 Chronicles 17:20-22 NIV).

He is the God who went toward his chosen people, Israel, to redeem them for himself. No other god did that. He made them his very own—forever. They belonged to God. Understanding and receiving their true identity as the object of God's affections provided God's ultimate protection and provision for their lives. It also gave them a holy purpose to live for his glory and his alone.

Sadly, many times God's people chose to forfeit their identity and foolishly ran after things that would never truly satisfy their hearts. God allowed it and the consequences that would naturally follow. Repentant, his people would eventually return to him. And because of his great mercy, he would once again receive them and declare his name over their lives.

His patience astounded me. God went to great lengths to warn and woo them back to himself. On day 52 of reading my Bible straight through, what I saw in Isaiah 49:16 took my breath away. "Look here. I have made you a part of Me, written you on the palms of My hands. Your city walls are always on My mind, always My concern" (THE VOICE). God made his people part of him. What a stunning picture of belonging.

I contemplated the fact that God carved them on the palm of his hand and always made them a matter of concern. I remember one day saying aloud, "Why can't they see it? Why do they always run away from their redeemer?"

But I knew exactly why. I run too. I saw my wayward heart smirking right back at me, as if I were looking in a mirror. God reminded me of the many times I had run from him as well. I too had chosen to make tiny gods over the one true God. I had also forgotten the many times he pursued my heart to bring me back. You see, he is the same yesterday, today, and forever (Hebrews 13:8). I learned that too.

After 67 days of reading through the Old Testament, the lengths God was willing to go to began to unfold right before my eyes. He came near. As their ever-tender and loving shepherd, he became like his people to bring them home once and for all. He knew them, and they would know him. I found this on day 76:

> My sheep hear my voice, and I know them, and they fol-
> low me. I give them eternal life, and they will never perish,

and no one will snatch them out of my hand. My Father, who has given them to me, is greater than all, and no one is able to snatch them out of the Father's hand. I and the Father are one (John 10:27-30).

He gives *his sheep* eternal life. He says we will never perish. He protects, provides, and gives purpose to the lives of his people. Only this time, in the flesh, through Jesus, they could see their names carved on the palm of his hands. He purchased their salvation once and for all and hung on the cross. There would be no mistaking the beautiful hands that would hold them tightly. He sealed the promise so that no one could ever take them out of his grasp. God gave his people to his beloved Son. Because he and the Father shared the same heart, they now belonged to Jesus too. Of course, they always had. Now they just saw it with their own eyes.

Dramatically, or so it seemed, after 21 days of reading the New Testament, Scripture nearly came to a grinding halt for me. It was like God pointed to Jesus and said, "Here is the way, the truth, and the life. He died for you. He conquered death. Follow him. Any questions? Good. Amen." His name was on every page from the beginning. The story of belonging had never been so clear to me. I wept at the thought, forever changed.

One of my favorite children's book authors, Sally Lloyd-Jones wrote,

> The Bible is most of all a Story…You see, the best thing about this story is—it's true. There are lots of stories in the Bible, but all the stories are telling one Big Story. The Story of how God loves his children and came to rescue them.
>
> It takes the whole Bible to tell this Story. And at the center of the Story, there is a baby. Every Story in the Bible whispers his name. He is like the missing piece in a puzzle—a piece that makes the other pieces fit together, and suddenly you can see a beautiful picture.[2]

We miss the beauty of the story and at times question God's declaration of love and promise of forever belonging to him. This started in

Nothing about
Jesus says rejection.

the garden when the Enemy slithered his way into the heart of God's beloved and sowed seeds of doubt. He said, "Did God really say…?" (Genesis 3:1 CEB), and we've been fearful of rejection—the very opposite of belonging—ever since. The Enemy has no real power over us, but he is crafty. He knows if he can get us doubting the Word of God we will forget our true identity. Once we forget who we are, we become vulnerable to drifting from the truth of whose we are. Like others before us, we miss the voice of our shepherd reminding us he is holding on to us and will never let us go.

Nothing about Jesus says rejection. He stands at the center of the story. He came to us. He invites us to lay down our weariness and find true rest. He sacrificed his life for our sins because we were helpless and lost on our own. He even prayed for us in his final hours and asked God to forgive his executioners. Today he sits on a throne of grace and mercy and continually intercedes for us (Hebrews 13:8; 7:25).

Ephesians tells part of the story too. It reveals a mystery so hidden in the heart of God that no one, not even Paul, had a clue. God's family was bigger and broader than previously thought. It included not only the nation of Israel, but others. Paul wrote,

> You had absolutely no connection to the Anointed; you were strangers, separated from God's people. You were aliens to the covenant they had with God; you were hopelessly stranded without God in a fractured world. But now, because of Jesus the Anointed and His sacrifice, all of that has changed. God gathered you who were so far away and brought you near to Him by the royal blood of the Anointed, our Liberating King (Ephesians 2:12-13 THE VOICE).

Brennan Manning wrote,

> What does Jesus do with hopelessly stranded outcasts? He invites them in. He gathers them close. And because of his sacrifice, they no longer belong to a fractured world. They who were without God now belong to him. He is the God

"who grabs scalawags and ragamuffins by the scruff of the neck and raises them up to seat them with princes and princesses of his people. Is this miracle enough for anybody? Or has the thunder of 'God so loved the world so much' been muffled by the roar of religious rhetoric that we are deaf to the word that God could have tender feelings for us?"[3]

> The truest thing about you is that you are his daughter. You belong to him. And nothing or no one—not even you—can snatch you out of his hand. His love for you is the best invitation you will ever get.

He does have tender feelings for you, my sweet friend. The truest thing about you is that you are his daughter. You belong to him. And nothing or no one—not even you—can snatch you out of his hand. His love for you is the best invitation you will ever get.

God is fiercely committed to repeating messages that are important to hearts that belong to him. He searches. He seeks. He supports. He always has (1 Chronicles 16:9). He says this over and over in his Word. He is saying it over and over in the book of Ephesians too. "This is Jesus," it says. "He is your identity. He redeemed you. He came for you and you belong to him." You can tuck yourself safely under the shelter of his wing. You are his. And you are home.

You Belong to a Family

The beauty of belonging to Jesus is enough. But God does more than we can ask for or imagine. By placing us in Christ, he has not only done something in us to secure our salvation; he has, as Charles Swindoll says, done "something between us."[4] God has brought us together into one family, forever:

> He is the embodiment of our peace, sent once and for all
> to take down the great barrier of hatred and hostility that

has divided us so that we can be one. He offered His body on the sacrificial altar to bring an end to the law's ordinances and dictations that separated Jews from the outside nations. His desire was to create in His body one new humanity from the two opposing groups, thus creating peace. Effectively the cross becomes God's means to kill off the hostility once and for all so that He is able to reconcile them both to God in this one new body (Ephesians 2:14-16 THE VOICE).

There have always been quarrels and divisions between different groups of people. For centuries, the greatest rift was between the Jews and Gentiles. The Jews followed the Law given by God and the Gentiles did not. This made the Gentiles unclean in the eyes of the Jewish people. They lived separate lives in every way.

The divine ordinances given by God to Israel stood as a wall between the Jews and other nations. In fact, there was a wall in the Jewish temple, separating the court of Gentiles from the rest of the temple areas. Archeologists have discovered the inscription from Herod's temple, and it reads like this: No foreigner may enter within the barricade which surrounds the sanctuary and enclosure. Anyone who is caught doing so will have himself to blame for his ensuing death.[5]

The Jews and the Gentiles were separated in every way. They even constructed a physical wall to ensure that division. Every Gentile knew ignoring the wall meant death. Jesus knew this too. His death effectively tore down the wall, because as the sufficient sacrifice for sins, he perfectly fulfilled the Law. The wall was no longer needed to separate us from God or each other, for that matter. And just to be clear that God was the one who took down the barrier, the veil in the temple tore from top to bottom:

At this point, it was about noon, and a darkness fell over the whole region. The darkness persisted until about three in the afternoon, and at some point during this darkness, the curtain in the temple was torn in two.

Jesus (shouting out loudly): Father, I entrust My spirit into Your hands!

And with those words, He exhaled—and breathed no more (Luke 23:44-46 THE VOICE).

There, hanging on the cross in the middle of darkness, Jesus is our peace and the temple curtain is demolished.

Can it be that simple? I love how Matthew Henry described what Christ, the embodiment of our peace, did. He said, "Sin breeds a quarrel between God and men. Christ came to take up the quarrel, and to bring it to an end, by reconciling both Jews and Gentiles, now collected and gathered into one body to a provoked and offended God."[6] We have no quarrel with God anymore. Jesus finished it on the cross. He has collected us and brought us together as one into his body. And as a result, we have no real quarrel with one another. Jesus reconciled us first to God.

The word *reconcile* means "in a literal sense to call back into union."[7] Now in perfect union with God, Christ goes one step further and reconciles us to one another. He did it by destroying everything we once used to keep one another at a distance. And then he started fresh and made us into one big family.

Standing on this side of the mystery, this may not seem like such a big deal. But I assure you, to the people of Ephesus this was a jaw-dropping part of the story they just couldn't seem to get over. I think each time they heard it they were in disbelief. I envision them scratching their heads, longing stirred within their hearts, saying quietly to one another, "Can this be true?"

Remarkably, it is. Take a closer look, and you'll see a shift happens between verses 13 and 14. Paul makes a shift from "you" to "us." The mystery isn't that you belong; it's that we all belong. We are equals embraced by Christ and able to embrace one another because of the cross. I love how Paul puts an exclamation point on the end of this section of his letter:

That's plain enough, isn't it? You're no longer wandering exiles. This kingdom of faith is now your home country. You're no longer strangers or outsiders. You *belong* here, with as much right to the name Christian as anyone. God is building a home. He's using us all—irrespective of how we got here—in what he is building. He used the apostles and prophets for the foundation. Now he's using you, fitting you in brick by brick, stone by stone, with Christ Jesus as the cornerstone that holds all the parts together. We see it taking shape day after day—a holy temple built by God, all of us built into it, a temple in which God is quite at home (Ephesians 2:19-22 MSG, emphasis added).

> The beauty of this mysterious new household of believers is that his dwelling is no longer behind a temple curtain he tore in two; it's within the sanctuary of our own hearts. He's building that sacred space as well. And he is quite at home there.

So here we stand, side by side, all pointing to Jesus as our reason for being part of his holy family. And while we can take all eternity to get over this grace-filled reality, God is using us all in what he is building—his household, or the church. Jesus, our cornerstone, holds us all together. Everyone plays a part, from the apostles and prophets, and now each one of us. The beauty of this mysterious new household of believers is that his dwelling is no longer behind a temple curtain he tore in two; it's within the sanctuary of our own hearts. He's building that sacred space as well. And he is quite at home there.

You Belong with a Purpose

Belonging to Jesus means we don't belong to the world. I'm grateful God didn't ask us to journey our way to heaven alone. We have brothers and sisters in Christ who are walking the same path, in the same direction:

> You were all called to travel on the same road and in the same direction, so stay together, both outwardly and inwardly. You have one Master, one faith, one baptism, one God and Father of all, who rules over all, works through all, and is present in all. Everything you are and think and do is permeated with Oneness (Ephesians 4:4-6 MSG).

Our goal as a family of faith brought together by Christ is oneness. But that doesn't mean we act the same or serve in the same way. Each one of us has been given a gift (verse 7) to use in the community of believers that exists to glorify God and bring us all to maturity—together. And this is our part:

- Equip God's people.

- Build up his body (the church).

- Be formed in his likeness.

- Stand mature in Christ.

Some of us will use our gifts to serve Christ and the church as apostles, prophets, evangelists, or shepherds, and others will be teachers. Everyone is needed, and no one is more important than the others. The goal is that the world we don't belong to (remember?) will not be able to toss us about and carry us away by half-truths and culturally popular religious-sounding whims. Together, walking the same path in the same direction with our eyes on Jesus, we won't be deceived so easily. And we will watch each other's back.

> The cross is the answer. Community is the context.

How do we do that? We speak the truth in love, and we grow in every way into Jesus, who is the head of the church (verse 15). Jesus is the one who joins and holds us together. "His very breath and blood flow through us, nourishing us so that we will grow up healthy in God, robust in love" (verse 16 MSG). Does it sound impossible? The cross is the answer. Community is the context:

> This is how God intends for us to live out our faith and love one another: in community. It is an incredible gift of God's grace to have a family faith. It is a gift of grace to gather corporately and stir up one another to faith and good works (Heb 10:24-25). It is a gift of grace to love one another as Christ loved us (John 13:34-35). It is a gift of grace to carry one another's burdens (Gal 6:2). It is a gift of grace to encourage one another and be encouraged by one another (1 Thess 5:11). It is a gift of grace to be taught and admonished by one another (Col 3:16). It is a gift of grace to be allowed the privilege to give financially to further the gospel (2 Cor 8-9). It is a gift of grace to come to the table for communion (1 Cor 11:26).
>
> All of these privileges have come to us via the cross-work of Jesus Christ. He has brought us near and made us one.[8]

Do you count the church a grace gift from the Father? I don't just mean the universal, worldwide church. I mean your local church. The people you do life with, your pastor who shepherds you, the girlfriends you meet for coffee, the worship team that leads you into the throne room—this is your grace gift to build you up and help you become like Christ. We need one another to grow, and we need one another when we're drowning in the hard things of everyday life.

Hand in Hand

Roberta Ursrey and her family were enjoying a day at Panama City Beach when her sons drifted too far from shore. The boys were in trouble, so good and dedicated mama that she was, Roberta grabbed her family and they swam to help the boys. But they too became victims of the strong rip current. Suddenly the family of nine was fighting for their lives. "I honestly thought I was going to lose my family that day," Ursrey said. "It was like, 'This is how I'm going.'"[9]

Luckily for the Ursrey family, the other beachgoers at Panama City Beach that day were not going to let that happen. Jessica Simmons and her family saw the Ursrey family struggling and heard their cries for help. They didn't have a rope, but they had each other. Her husband was the one to suggest, "Let's grab hand to hand, wrist to wrist out to them, and the person on the end can grab them and we can pull each other back in."

That is exactly what they did. Stretching 100 yards or so out into the waters of the Gulf, with the tallest men on the end in neck-deep water, 30 people linked hands to save this family. Jessica said after the successful rescue, "Yes, it was dangerous, but who is going to actually sit on a beach and watch someone drown? I mean, I'm not. So you gotta do what you gotta do…creating a chain was our best resource."[10]

This past year my family was drowning too. Not in the ocean, but in another life-and-death situation with my husband in the ICU. My local church formed a similar human chain and grabbed onto our wrists and pulled us safely to shore. They refused to leave us alone in our impossible moments. They said, just like my friend Robin did years ago, "You belong here." They didn't sit by and watch us be overwhelmed by waves of adversity. They got into the water with us, and they held on for dear life.

The body of Christ is filled with imperfect people all walking in the same path in the same direction. We may not always get it right. But it can be beautiful. It is beautiful. Jesus made it so.

BIBLE STUDY

Encouragement

Ephesians 4:4-14

Connection

1. Share one statement from the chapter that was most significant to you and why.

2. Tell about a time when you felt like you belonged. What made a difference for you?

3. What does it mean to you that Christ's death on the cross tore down the dividing wall between us?

4. What part in the body of Christ have you been called to play?

Growth

1. If you don't know what your spiritual gifts are, how you might contribute to your local church body, discover them. You can take tests online or ask your church leadership to help you identify your gifts.

2. Memorize Ephesians 4:4-6 (ESV): There is one body and one Spirit—just as you were called to the one hope that belongs to your call—one Lord, one faith, one baptism, one God and Father of all, who is over all and through all and in all.

My Notes:

_____

_____

_____

_____

_____

_____

4

Bow the Knee

God is radically committed to my life of prayer. He shed the blood of His Son so that I might be cleansed and rendered fit to stand before Him in love.

MILTON VINCENT[1]

Key Scriptures: Ephesians 1:15-23; Ephesians 3:14-21; Ephesians 6:18; 2 Kings 6:15-17; 1 Corinthians 13

We must have stood in the store for 30 minutes or more, laughing so hard we caused a scene. We had ducked into a shop my friend wanted to peruse quickly, only to find a wall of quotes and jokes on tiny wooden blocks that caused us to come undone in the best way. A few of my favorites were:

Relax. We're all crazy and it's not a competition.

I prefer not to think before speaking. I like to be as surprised as everyone else by what comes out of my mouth.

I laughed so hard tears ran down my leg.

Soon, other groups of shoppers stood near us to see what kept us from being quiet. I think they might have had more fun laughing at us than with us. But we didn't care. We're used to it. We took turns picking our very own "life" quote and taking a picture for our fearless group leader, Lisa. I still have those pictures on my phone, and I giggle when I scroll by them.

This is just one of the memories we jotted down in our reunion book this year. We've been adding seemingly insignificant hilarious events to this annual for 25 years. We all met at Indiana University and have some connection through Lisa. Some of us were in her Bible study during our college years. Others were in a connecting group led by one of her girls. I just happened to be in the right place at the right time to be grafted in over two decades ago. This year, we spent a wonderful weekend in Nashville eating our way through town and catching up. There was much to catch up on too. The first night all eight of us were together, we stayed up until 2:00 a.m., talking, crying, and praying. The next morning we remembered why, after all these years, we shouldn't do that anymore. We aren't as young as we used to be. I treasure our times together, and I always leave our gatherings with a heart full of joy.

The older I get, the more I realize friendships might be born out of a sweet moment of discovery and understanding between two individuals, but they survive because of grit. It has certainly taken grit for eight women who live in eight different places across the country to get together once each year for a weekend. But we think it's worth it, no matter what.

What is grit? you might be asking. Angela Lee Duckworth discussed grit in her 2013 TED Talk, now viewed over 11 million times:

> Grit is passion and perseverance for very long-term goals. Grit is having stamina. Grit is sticking with your future, day in, day out, not just for the week, not just for the month, but for years, and working really hard to make that future a reality. Grit is living life like it's a marathon, not a sprint.[2]

We decided a long time ago to stick together as a group of friends, not just for a short time, but for the marathon of life. It hasn't been easy, but with sheer determination and the grit to keep going, we've managed to stay together. And the rewards just keep getting sweeter.

I want to be "gritty" about other things in life that really matter, like relationships, my walk with Jesus, and my writing, to name a few. The good thing is that it doesn't seem to be based on how good I am at these things naturally. Duckworth goes on to say, "What I do know is that talent doesn't make you gritty. Our data show very clearly that there are many talented individuals who simply do not follow through on their commitments. In fact, in our data, grit is usually unrelated or even inversely related to measures of talent."[3] I can be good at being gritty and not give up. Talent is wonderful, but grit might get me there too.

I know I need to apply this grit mentality to my prayer life. It seems to me I go through seasons when prayer is at the forefront of my mind and I'm purposeful in it every day. But sometimes my prayer times come few and far between, which adds to my feeling disconnected to my Savior. I don't want to do that anymore.

I recently had a conversation about this very thing with one of my friends from that group of eight college friends. She emailed me a few deep thoughts that rang true in my heart. Maybe you can relate too. (As an aside, her comment about her hair is just one of our ongoing conversations and only adds to the true nature of our friendship. We go back and forth about all types of things and never miss a beat.) She wrote:

> I'm drinking the dregs of my reheated coffee as I type. This would be way better if we were face-to-face. Then you could see how LARGE my hair is in the humidity. LARGE.
>
> I have been thinking about prayer a lot. I'm largely (like my hair) bad at it. I want to pray. I want to talk with God—unceasingly, freely, intimately. I also want to intercede for friends and family and the world and talk to God about things that are on God's heart, like the nasty stuff going on in the world, the souls of men and women, and suffering brothers and sisters. I tend to think of prayer and intercession differently...devotionally praying is different in my mind than praying FOR someone or something. I could be wrong...I think it has to do with the practicalities of actually making it happen. When do I do it? When do I intercede for THE WORLD?

Do you see why we're friends? Coffee. Bad hair. Jesus. I want to have this conversation face-to-face too, but since she lives in Michigan and I live in Orlando, we make do. That is what girlfriends do. I love her so much for her honesty. I feel bad at praying most days too. My friend went on to say,

> I pray in fits and starts, there are "good" seasons and "bad" seasons. It's possible that I view prayer wrongly—as something to DO rather than as an invitation to join God. Nonetheless, there remains a doing on my part. Prayer is active. Intercession is ACTIVE—it requires intentionality, time, practice, even sacrifice (dare I use that word?) of time spent doing something else.

I feel like I pray in fits and starts too. Do you? God has been working in my heart regarding prayer. I'm seeing that prayer is born out of my relationship *with* God through Jesus. Is it possible that my prayer life is more of a reflection of the fits and starts of my relationship with God? That is entirely painful to admit. The Father who blessed and blesses me is inviting me, through grace, to a place of belonging that yields a life that can't help but burst forth a constant conversation with him. This is made possible only because of the sacrifice of his Son. Jesus, of course, modeled this beautifully in his earthly life. He is the same yesterday, today, and forever, and right now he lives to intercede on behalf of those who draw near to him (Hebrews 17:25).

Andrew Murray wrote,

> Of all the traits of a life like Christ, there is none higher and more glorious than conformity to Him in the work that now engages Him without ceasing in the Father's presence: His all-powerful intercession. The more we abide in Him and grow to be like Him, the more His priestly life will work in us. Our lives will become what His is: a life that continuously prays for men.[4]

Do you know who doesn't pray in fits and starts? Jesus. The work he engages in unceasingly today is prayer. Prayer is an invitation to join

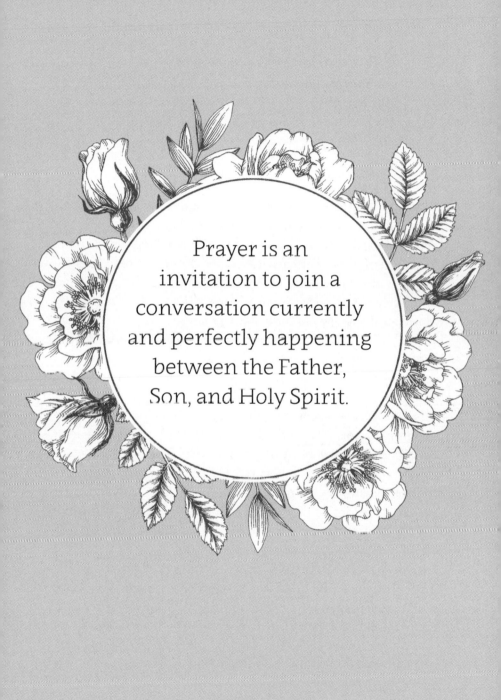

Prayer is an invitation to join a conversation currently and perfectly happening between the Father, Son, and Holy Spirit.

a conversation currently and perfectly happening between the Father, Son, and Holy Spirit. And when I look at it that way, I wonder why I wouldn't beg to be part of that unceasingly. The beautiful part of being his girl is I don't have to beg—the offer to participate is always available to me. I think Jesus is waiting for us to say yes to this glorious invitation. Divinely planned for us, Ephesians is a perfect place to be reminded of these very truths.

Prayer in Ephesians

Paul's abiding love for Jesus and his affection for his friends in Ephesus caused his heart to overflow with prayer more than once in this letter. In so many ways, Ephesians feels like one long prayer to me. It's Paul's most prayer-saturated letter. James Rosscup wrote, "Despite being only about one-third the length of Romans, Ephesians has proportionately more than 55% as many verses directly related to prayer."[5] Remember the weepy hot mess of tears that fell when Paul departed Ephesus for the last time? His final act of love and devotion was to bend his knee and pray over his friends. What did he pray for them? We don't know. But I would guess the words he wrote in his letter sang a similar tune.

I recently had the chance to speak at my church for our first women's ministry event of the year, called Girls' Night Out. Before it started, each of the 30 or so women who would be leading table discussions gathered around me to pray over me as well as the women walking in the doors that night. They placed their loving hands on me and began to intercede boldly. As they prayed I fought back tears. Their words were beautiful. But as soon as it was over, I couldn't remember much of what they said in that holy moment.

I wonder if Paul's friends in Ephesus experienced the same thing. Finally, with the arrival of his letter to their community, Paul doesn't leave his friends straining to remember his words on the boat before he left. This time he wrote them down.

Paul's Prayer for Understanding

> Because I have heard of your faith in the Lord Jesus and
> your love toward all the saints, I do not cease to give thanks
> for you, remembering you in my prayers, that the God of
> our Lord Jesus Christ, the Father of glory, may give you the
> Spirit of wisdom and of revelation in the knowledge of him,
> having the eyes of your hearts enlightened, that you may
> know what is the hope to which he has called you, what
> are the riches of his glorious inheritance in the saints, and
> what is the immeasurable greatness of his power toward us
> who believe, according to the working of his great might
> that he worked in Christ when he raised him from the dead
> and seated him at his right hand in the heavenly places, far
> above all rule and authority and power and dominion, and
> above every name that is named, not only in this age but
> also in the one to come. And he put all things under his feet
> and gave him as head over all things to the church, which
> is his body, the fullness of him who fills all in all (Ephe-
> sians 1:15-23).

Paul is like a proud spiritual father in this passage. I don't think he
can help praying and thanking the Lord for the work God has initi-
ated in the lives of the Ephesians. Word that the Ephesians are serving God and loving one another has reached him all the way in Rome.

It wasn't as though Paul could look at the Facebook feed of the
church at Ephesus. This report had to be brought to him in person
from someone who knew it firsthand. Probably he'd been waiting for
this report from the time he left them. I can imagine the joy and gratitude he felt in light of his final warning to them: "I know that after
my departure fierce wolves will come in among you, not sparing the
flock; and from among your own selves will arise men speaking twisted
things, to draw away the disciples after them" (Acts 20:29-30).

No wonder Paul doesn't stop thanking God and praying for those
he invested in so dearly. I feel the same way when I catch my daughters

doing something right. *Did you just help your sister get ready for bed? Were you cheering her on when she was discouraged? Did you really sit up late and listen to her tell you story after story when you'd rather be asleep?* "Thank you, Lord!" I'll say when I hear and see evidence of sisterly affection bubble up in their lives. In a world gone crazy, these four girls are going to need one another. Essentially, Paul is doing the same thing as he constantly remembers the Ephesians. I don't think he can help himself.

I've heard it said that nothing makes you love a person more than praying for them. Paul couldn't help praying for the Ephesians because he loved them. That he loved them because he prayed for them is also true. What did Paul pray for those he loved?

Wisdom, revelation, and knowledge of God

First, notice Paul asks that "the God of our Lord Jesus Christ, the Father of glory" (Ephesians 1:17), the same God whom he has blessed and who has already blessed the Ephesians, would do still more for them. Don't miss this: God wants us to ask him for wisdom and knowledge. He delights in answering this prayer. He desires to reveal himself to his children.

Notice how Paul is praying and teaching at the same time. We don't have to be preaching from a pulpit to teach. So often when I've listened to prayer warriors, I've wanted to write down what they said because it was a profound truth of God. They knew something about God I wanted to know and experience as well. I think this is one of the hidden blessings of prayer. Matthew Henry wrote, "He has laid up these spiritual blessings for us in the hands of his Son, the Lord Jesus; but then he has appointed us to draw them out, and fetch them in, by prayer. We have no part nor lot in the matter, any further than we claim it by faith and prayer."[6] The very truths Paul has just preached over the Ephesians in the previous 14 verses are best drawn out into our daily lives through prayer.

We have a habit of going to God with our upload of requests and needs. And that's fine: Paul reminds us in Philippians 4:6-8 that we are welcome to present our requests to God. But God wants us to draw near and draw out who he is in our lives. He wants to download more than we can imagine through a deeper knowledge and revelation of his character. True character in Christ is already waiting for us to grasp and possess by understanding.

All our lives—all our experiences—have been an appeal from God to know him. He has wooed us, won us, and walked with us through every chapter of life. He wants us to know him. Can you imagine God denying such a request? I can't. After all, it's his idea.

The eyes of hearts enlightened

Knowing gives way to seeing, and Paul wants the Ephesians to have a vision nothing short of heavenly anchored. He asks God to allow them to see differently, perhaps differently than they ever have before, not seeing the physical but the spiritual. He knows the Spirit of God is the one who opens our hearts to clear understanding. This reminds me of the story of Elisha and his servant in 2 Kings. Elisha prayed a prayer of enlightenment too. Just look how God answered his prayer:

> When the servant of the man of God rose early in the morning and went out, behold, an army with horses and chariots was all around the city. And the servant said, "Alas, my master! What shall we do?" He said, "Do not be afraid, for those who are with us are more than those who are with them." Then Elisha prayed and said, "O LORD, please open his eyes that he may see." So the Lord opened the eyes of the young man, and he saw, and behold, the mountain was full of horses and chariots of fire all around Elisha" (2 Kings 6:15-17).

Elisha and his servant were surrounded by the enemy. But Elisha wasn't afraid. He knew God was present, and that they weren't outnumbered, but surrounded in an entirely different way. He prayed, "O Eternal One, I ask You to allow my servant to see heavenly realities"

(2 Kings 6:17 THE VOICE). God answered the prayer, and suddenly the servant had eyes to see clearly what was happening on a grander scale.

What a beautiful picture of what Paul is also praying. He wants the Ephesians to see heavenly realities too. He wants them to truly know

- the hope to which he has called us.

- the riches of his glorious inheritance in the saints.

- the immeasurable greatness of his power toward us who believe.

These are not pretty little boxes to check off. Paul wants them to *know* these things as surely as they know their names. He wants them to see greater things than physical eyes can see. He longs for God to let them see with their hearts.

These are heavenly realities for us as well. God, Father of our Lord Jesus Christ, has called us all to embrace with joyful expectation our salvation, which is both future and current. There is great hope in knowing one day we will experience in full our glorious inheritance, when Jesus comes back to rescue us and take us safely home. We are truly surrounded with an abundance of blessings to come. They are ours in Christ already—he is safely keeping them in heaven for us.

But this verse also highlights that God has an inheritance in us. Notice that verse 18 says, "What are the riches of *his* glorious inheritance in the saints" (emphasis mine). As Warren Wiersbe tells us,

> This is an amazing truth—that a God should look on us as part of His great wealth. Just as man's wealth brings glory to his name, so God will get glory from the church because of what He has invested in us. When Jesus Christ returns we shall be "to the praise of the glory of his grace"[7] (Ephesians 1:6 KJV).

God has an inheritance in you, and you bring glory to his name because of it.

Fixing our eyes on Jesus and this truth can keep us running on the days we would like to sit down by the road and just weep.

Magnificently, this broken world isn't the end. Girls, we get to run home with hope. Can you see it? But in the meantime, all we have is not merely future-related. Remember the deposit he's placed within us in the person of the Holy Spirit? This down payment comes with power. And not just any power, but the same power that raised Christ from the dead. In Ephesians 1:19-21, Paul says,

> What is the immeasurable greatness of his power toward us who believe, according to the working of his great might that he worked in Christ when he raised him from the dead and seated him at his right hand in the heavenly places, far above all rule and authority and power and dominion, and above every name that is named, not only in this age but also in the one to come.

The Greek word here for "power" happens to be my favorite Greek word. It's *dynamis*: "Inherent power, power residing in a thing by virtue of its nature, or which a person or a thing exerts and puts forth."[8] Our word *dynamite* has its origins here. Think of it like this: All the power a stick of dynamite needs to explode is within it. The power Paul is talking about, which lives inside you, *raised* Christ from the dead. Now, that's explosive, right?

> This is our hope: Heaven is coming, and today you have all the power you need in the Holy Spirit to live out your calling until you get there.

This is our hope: Heaven is coming, and today you have all the power you need in the Holy Spirit to live out your calling until you get there. We are rich, my sweet friends, and it spills over today and on into heaven.

Do you know how much you mean to Christ? We lack nothing we need. We are rich indeed. Do you know it? Do you believe it? Paul was praying the Ephesians would. And I'm praying we do too.

I think it's interesting to note what Paul *doesn't* pray for the Ephesians. He doesn't ask God to give them physical blessings. He doesn't ask him to take away their trials or remove any persecutions they may face. Coming from a pastor sitting in a prison cell, this is rich. Paul doesn't want his friends to be spared from anything that may help these truths dig down deep into their hearts. Our earthly circumstances make us run to Jesus and draw out those spiritual blessings that are ours. Truthfully, we often don't seek them until we have nothing left to cling to. But when we do seek them, we find these blessings in Christ are for us both today and when we are seated securely in Christ in the heavenly places where nothing and no one is above him forever and ever. Amen.

Paul's Prayer for Power

> I bow my knees before the Father, from whom every family in heaven and on earth is named, that according to the riches of his glory he may grant you to be strengthened with power through his Spirit in your inner being, so that Christ may dwell in your hearts through faith—that you, being rooted and grounded in love, may have strength to comprehend with all the saints what is the breadth and length and height and depth, and to know the love of Christ that surpasses knowledge, that you may be filled with all the fullness of God (Ephesians 3:14-19).

I stood in her kitchen eating a handful of candy corn and peanuts, soaking up the encouragement my friend Lisa so easily handed out. I was avoiding the obvious and acting as though my husband was not in our van, waiting for me to come back in the five minutes I had promised. She was our last stop on our way out of town. We were moving our little family south, and I was picking up a box of maternity clothes that would be just what I needed for warmer weather.

"You're going to be fine. You're going to be *great*."

I teared up, and she hugged me.

"Really? Do you think so?" I choked out.

"I know it."

Lisa was helping me do the bravest thing I had ever done—start a new life in Florida, away from my whole community. At least 15 minutes later, with my husband still patiently waiting for me, she gave me one final hug, blessed me with a short prayer, and sent me on my way.

I cried for miles.

Lisa has always been the kind of girlfriend who keeps me moving toward Jesus, believing he has good plans for me, even when I can't see it myself. She also taught me about the importance of prayer becoming a habit—mostly that you don't need to make a big deal over when and how you engage in prayer. Sometimes you simply need to break out and pray when the moment calls for it. Lisa often did this while we were driving around town.

I remember the first time she had one of these prayer moments. We were picking up Chinese food (her favorite), and I was telling her some tale of woe in my life. Without so much as a warning, she started praying in the car. She didn't even tell me she was going to pray. It was as though she exhaled a prayer instead of her next breath. When she finished she said, "Stace, God has you. And I'll keep praying." It was the first time I'd ever heard someone talk to God as though the conversation was already happening. I now do this with my girls as we drive back and forth to school, and dance, and, of course, the grocery store. And it makes me miss Lisa every time.

Paul prayed like breathing too. He prayed in person. He wrote out his prayers. He prayed specifically. He broke out into prayer—like Lisa; he couldn't help himself. He was a man fiercely committed to pray for those he was leading. He commented on this when he said at the end of his letter to the Ephesians, "Pray always. Pray in the Spirit. Pray about everything in every way you know how! And keeping all this in mind, pray on behalf of God's people. Keep on praying feverishly, and be on the lookout until evil has been stayed" (Ephesians 6:18 THE VOICE). Paul prayed feverishly because he knew it was vital not only to those he prayed for, but also for his own heart.

Do you notice that the most dedicated prayer warriors tend to know God deeply? They are the ones who draw near and ask of him. They don't stop praying, and in the process they grow to look like Jesus. Do you want to know God and become like him too? Oh, girls, we must know him in prayer.

In Paul's second prayer in Ephesians chapter 3, he starts to pray and then interrupts himself. He inserts his story in verses 2-13. He didn't edit his letter to make it flow seamlessly. I think Paul is imagining he's sitting with his beloved Ephesian friends and having a true conversation with them. Maybe like me, he verbalizes what he's writing and then thinks aloud, "Oh, I shouldn't assume they know this about my calling. I'd better just add it in here." I understand that all Scripture is breathed out by God (2 Timothy 3:16), and I love that this part is left in. It's both important (as we discussed in chapter 2) and shows that this letter was written by a real person who passionately wrote and prayed for his friends.

As we move into the second half of the letter, Paul is going to shift *from being who we are in Christ* to the *(be)havior that overflows from a heart that is his*. And parked in the middle of these two sections of Paul's letter is a prayer about the power we need to know and experience.

Paul's prayer for spiritual strength and power starts from a position of great humility. We've already witnessed this posture of prayer by Paul when he left the Ephesians in Acts 20. He bowed his knee there among his friends as well. This is worth noting, because it wasn't typical for Jews to pray in this way. "Kneeling," Tony Merida wrote, "was not common for Jews. The typical position was one of standing, as we see today at the Wailing Wall. Whenever someone is kneeling in prayer in the Bible, he is indicating deep humility and deep emotion before God.[9]

Paul is deeply emotional before God, probably for two reasons. First, he has just used the first part of his letter to remind them of their worth in Christ and the amazing grace that made this all possible. They are united as one in Christ, and this is reason enough to take a knee to pray in gratitude and heartfelt worship.

I also think Paul bows his knee in prayer because he sees himself in true humility. Remember, he said, "To me, *though I am the very least of all the saints*, this grace was given, to preach to the Gentiles the unsearchable riches of Christ" (Ephesians 3:7-8, emphasis mine). No wonder he bowed his knee in prayer. Even if he prostrated himself, I don't think Paul could get low enough to show his adoration of Christ and his deep emotion over these faithful believers.

Paul's life was marked by prayer. He loved the Ephesians. Clearly, that love was put there by God, and he was desperate for God to answer his requests on their behalf. Tony Merida posed a question: "Why is Paul so passionate and desperate in Ephesians 3:14? I think because he knows what the Ephesians need is something that only comes from God: power. Notice how Paul prays that God would 'grant' them to be strengthened (verse 16). He knew God's power was a gift so he was desperate for God to answer."[10]

> When you find yourself needing something
> only God can give, you get on your knees
> and ask him. There is no other way.

What makes you get on your knees? What breaks your heart? What moves you with a desperate passion to pray without ceasing? Maybe it has been awhile since you humbly bent your knees to cry out to God for anything. When you find yourself needing something only God can give, you get on your knees and ask him. There is no other way.

Do you know what I've found when my knees have hit the floor before God the Father? He always meets me there in the sweetest way. He lifts my face, draws me near, and listens to my heart.

I experienced this last February when my husband was admitted to the ICU. That first night, I couldn't get low enough to cry out to the Lord. I found myself on the floor as sobs wracked my body, a Bible open to Psalm 23. I must have laid there for an hour or more, desperately seeking his face. I found, in the most extraordinary way, that my desperation doesn't cause Jesus to flee; it draws him like nothing else. What he did in my heart over the next few days and weeks mirrors exactly what Paul prayed for his friends. I was strengthened with power, rooted in love, filled with the fullness of God, and I watched in awe as he did more than I could ask for or imagine. God still answers these prayers, because they are his words and his ideas.

Strengthened in Power

> God doesn't run out of strength—ever. His storehouse is never low. We have an eternal and ongoing power source that has nothing do with our power. It all comes from God.

Paul is bowing his knee in desperate humility, but even in his humility he knows he can ask confidently for God to continue the work he's started. Keep in mind that Paul has been writing to them about these true things. Now he's praying they will experience them personally. Paul asks that God would give them inward strength out of his abundance. God doesn't run out of strength—ever. His storehouse is never low. We have an eternal and ongoing power source that has nothing do with our power. It all comes from God.

I experienced this a millionfold when Mike was in the hospital. So many people would say to me, "How are you standing here? I couldn't do this." My response was, "I'm not. This is not me." My legs were so weak I couldn't truly stand on my own. Each step I took was pulled from the inward power I was drawing from God.

How does he do that? God dwells within our hearts through the Holy Spirit. His plan for us is for his presence to pervade us and transform us into his image. Part of prayer is acknowledging that presence and inviting God to feel at home in our hearts to stay and truly make us his own. And this was exactly what Paul was praying and teaching his friends they could pray too.

Rooted in Love

Paul knew his readers could be rooted in a lot of things. They might have been tempted to be firmly established financially, or by their lofty position in society. Yet when he bowed his knee and prayed passionately for his friends, he asked God to grant them stability in the steady strength and character of divine love.

Paul knew about love. He echoed this in his letter to the Corinthian church (written from the city of Ephesus, remember?). He said without love we have nothing because

- love is totally other-centered.

- love rejoices with the truth.

- love bears and believes when everything else fails.

- love doesn't lose heart.

- love doesn't end.

"Faith, hope, and love abide, these three; but the greatest of these is love" (1 Corinthians 13:13). Of all the things that endure and continue forever, the *agape* love of God is the greatest. Paul was reminding them of this anchoring love that took Jesus to the cross on their behalf. But he didn't stop there. He asked God to make them able to comprehend this love on a deep level.

The word for "comprehend" in the Greek language is *katalambano*, and it means "to lay hold of, to make one's own, to seize and take possession of."[11] He wanted them to lay hold of the exact nature of God's love for them and let it fill them up entirely. The imagery here for "fullness" is like a ship that is filled or manned with soldiers.[12]

Have you ever watched a sailing competition on the high seas? The sailors are in constant motion, working together to keep the ship afloat and propel it forward. God's love is like that for believers—always working for us. But even our ability to understand it and grab hold of it is a gift from God.

This prayer always makes me want to cry, because I often pray it for my girls. I see their faces when I read these words of Paul inspired by the Holy Spirit:

> May [he] grant you to be strengthened with power through his Spirit in your inner being, so that Christ may dwell in your hearts through faith—that you, being rooted and grounded in love, may have strength to comprehend with all the saints what is the breadth and length and height and depth, and to know the love of Christ that surpasses knowledge, that you may be filled with all the fullness of God (Ephesians 3:16-19).

I have no doubt whatsoever that if my girls truly grab hold of God's love for them and understand it to the depths of their souls, they will never settle for the world's cheap knockoff. They won't want to be loved for what they do or how they act. They will be firmly fixed in a love that marched to the cross and died in their place. They will see a sacrificial love that drew them out of their sinfulness and rescued them when they were unlovable at best. They will walk in this love knowing they are held firmly in its grip and that it will never let them go. I can't think of a better prayer to pray.

The Amen

Paul closes not only his prayer but the first part of his letter with a hymn of praise giving glory to God. I don't think he can help himself. Don't you just love Paul's enthusiasm throughout this letter? I love that as we read his holy, inspired words, we catch a glimpse of his heart as well. I wonder if the Ephesians caught the smile in his voice as they read these next couple of sentences and said to themselves, "Here he goes again." And their love for him and Jesus only got stronger as he declared,

> Now to him who is able to do far more abundantly than all that we ask or think, according to the power at work within us, to him be glory in the church and in Christ Jesus throughout all generations, forever and ever. Amen (Ephesians 3:20-21).

Notice a couple of things Paul says here:

First, *God can do above and beyond* what we can ask for or even think about asking for.

Second, *God is already at work in us through Christ.* We don't have to wish for it. It is happening now.

> We may fetch the richness of God's grace and mercy
> in prayer, but we can never drain God of it.

Let this encourage your heart today and then again tomorrow. Matthew Henry said, "There is an inexhaustible fullness of grace and mercy in God, which the prayers of all the saints can never draw dry. Whatever we ask, or think to ask, still God is able to do more, abundantly more, exceedingly abundantly more."[13] We may fetch the richness of God's grace and mercy in prayer, but we can never drain God of it.

Think of it this way: When you are weary, he is not. When you feel like you can't love one more person, God is just getting started. If you are faithless, he is faithful. When you want to quit, he has endless energy and power to keep running. All that you need, he already has. And then he has more. Glory. This makes me want to pray as well.

God, you want us to know you. You bring us into your family. You give us your name—a name that is true and rich and everlasting. No one can change that name. We are your daughters. And then you lay a rich foundation of love. You root us there. You love and love and love. You pour it out so deep that we have the chance to grow in it forever.

But you don't stop there. You extend the invitation to be known. Some leaders don't always want to be truly known. They withhold parts of their story; they show us only the parts they want us to know.

But you don't do that. You are an open book—literally with your Word. With an extended hand you tell us to explore who you are. You delight in us knowing you.

You give us your worth through Christ.

Your grace makes us who we are.

You put us in your family, a place of belonging forever.

May we endeavor to know you, to search out these riches all the days of our lives, and to live in that love. Let it flow from you to us to others. That love is the truest love there is. I know it is true for us. I know it is available. I believe that if we truly do lay hold of it, we would not let go. Because you won't let us go—ever.

WITH—A Way to Pray

This study of Ephesians has truly marked me for good. And as I'm working my way through the pages of the letter again, I can't help but think prayer may be one of the application points I find myself rehearsing over and over.

As I am immersed in prayer, God has been confirming this truth in my heart: Jesus is at his right hand already in constant conversation *with* him about the things that concern me. When I step into that conversation, I don't have to tell him what's happening, what I'm feeling, or what my greatest fear is. He knows. The absolute beauty of this truth is it takes the focus off me and allows me to look full in the face of the One I desperately want to be like. I don't have to conjure up the conversation; it is already happening. I'm already seated with him, invited into a conversation that is ongoing.

Here's what the WITH prayer model is all about:

W—Worship

> Worshiping God frees us to understand at a heart
> level that we are not responsible for all things.
> We don't hold the world together by the power of
> our word. Jesus does that by the power of his word.

The appropriate response to God's invitation to be in prayerful conversation with him is to recognize who he is and tell him. We do this through worship.

Anytime we come face-to-face with who God is, his attributes, or who he has revealed himself to be in his Word, the experience has the power to change us. As we worship God, he increases, and we decrease.

Worshiping God frees us to understand at a heart level that we are not responsible for all things. We don't hold the world together by the power of our word. Jesus does that by the power of his word (Hebrews 1:3).

But don't be confused. God already knows who he is. Your worship serves as a reminder for you to remember him, rightly. Consider this from Andrew Murray: "God is a God who hides Himself to the carnal eye. As long as in our worship of God we are chiefly occupied with our own thoughts and exercises, we will not meet Him Who is Spirit, the Unseen One. But to the man who withdraws himself from all that is of the world and man and waits for God alone, the Father will reveal Himself. As he shuts out the world and its life, surrendering himself to be led by Christ into God's presence, the light of the Father's love will fall on him."[14]

Is it possible that worship allows us to withdraw from ourselves and the world around us and enter into the presence of God in a powerful way? It would seem Paul thought so and modeled this as he prayed.

I tend to call out in God the very part of his character that I most need at the time. My worship pastor said as much the other night at choir practice when he asked, "When we worship God and affirm his attributes, does he lean into that part of who he is and reveal it to a greater degree as we seek him?" I think perhaps he does.

David—shepherd, worship leader, anointed king—modeled this type of worshipful prayer often in the book of Psalms. We can catch a glimpse of his needful worship, calling out and reminding his own heart of who God is when we read:

> The Lord is my light and my salvation;
>> whom shall I fear?
> The Lord is the stronghold of my life;
>> of whom shall I be afraid?
>
> When evildoers assail me
>> to eat up my flesh,
>> my adversaries and foes,
>> it is they who stumble and fall.
>
> Though an army encamp against me,
>> my heart shall not fear;
> though war arise against me,
>> yet I will be confident (Psalm 27:1-3).

I think David had a real fear of his enemies who wanted him destroyed. I think he was surrounded by them. He cried out in prayer to the Lord who was his:

Light
Salvation
Stronghold
Confidence

And as he drew toward this image of God and sought the face of the Lord, he was heard. Look at his final declaration in this passage:

> I believe that I shall look upon the goodness of the Lord
>> in the land of the living!
> Wait for the Lord;
>> be strong, and let your heart take courage;
>> wait for the Lord! (Psalm 27:13-14).

God lifted David's head, encouraged his heart, and gave him courage because of who *he* is. Would the Lord do less for you and me?

> Oh, Lord, let the light of your love fall
> on us in the places we need most.

I—*In Christ*

With our worship of God declared and his position rightly affirmed, it's time for us to remember our position as well. Over and over in the book of Ephesians, Paul reminds us that we are *in Christ*. We need to come to the Father, recognizing our position in Christ, our need of him, and the forgiveness he has given us for our sins.

This is a place in our conversation with God where we rehearse the truth of the gospel. I know I need to do that every day. Without Christ, where would I be? I'd have no access, no advocate, no ability to save myself whatsoever. Now seated in Christ as God's daughter, I have all those things and more. Galatians 2:20 says, "I have been crucified with Christ. It is no longer I who live, but Christ who lives in me. And the life I now live in the flesh I live by faith in the Son of God, who loved me and gave himself for me." I am both seated in Christ and he is living in me. Through the power of his Spirit, he is continually making me like him. My life is his and no longer mine. Rightly seated in a place he has victoriously won, I'm able to receive exactly what I need.

T—*Teach Us to Pray*

I love that the 12 men who followed Jesus while he walked on this earth were normal, everyday guys who probably didn't have any training in Scripture other than what their mothers and fathers had taught them. They really meant it when they said in Luke 11:1, "Lord, teach us to pray." They wanted to learn from him. Do I need any less?

The model of the Lord's Prayer, which follows their request, is worth imitating to be sure. You will see worship, confession, and petition in his words. As we approach him similarly, we can simply ask, "Jesus, what are you already praying for me in this situation?"

We can be certain that the prayer God bends to is never out of agreement with his Word, so a good place to learn how to pray is in Scripture.

These two prayers in Ephesians, among others, are great places to start. You might begin by simply reading the prayers aloud and inserting your name (or the names of others) where appropriate. I do this all the time when I come to a verse or passage I especially want to be true in my life or the lives of others I love. For example, in one of the Ephesians prayers, it might sound like this when I pray for my husband:

> *Father, out of your honorable and glorious riches, strengthen Mike. Fill his soul with the power of your Spirit so that through faith the Anointed One will reside in Mike's heart. May love be the rich soil where his life takes root. May it be the bedrock where Mike's life is founded so that together with all your people, Mike will have the power to understand that the love of the Anointed is infinitely long, wide, high, and deep, surpassing everything anyone previously experienced. God, may your fullness flood through Mike's entire being." (This is based on Ephesians 3:16-19, THE VOICE.)*

Another place to consider looking is how Jesus prayed for us. I wrote about this in some length in *Is Jesus Worth It?* But you can also turn to John 17 and read what is often referred to as The High Priestly Prayer of Jesus. These are some of the precious last words Christ said before he was taken to be crucified. That he spent his time praying for himself, his followers, and those who would come to know him later (like you and me) is breathtaking. We can learn so much about a heart for prayer when we study and reflect on his words.

Also, I think praying Scripture back to God is akin to what my kids do when they come to me and say, "Mom, you said…" I don't usually argue with what I said. God's Word teaches us to pray in a way that honors God and his truth. It brings our own thoughts and intentions in alignment with his. As we pray, his Word becomes part of our prayer language as well, and I think that's a beautiful by-product. We sound like him with his words in our mouths. Oh, it must be music to his ears.

H—Help

With our gratitude and worship aligning us with the heart of God, our position rightly remembered as seated in the place of victory in Christ, and a heartfelt request to be taught to pray through the power of the Spirit and the living, active, sharp Word of God, we go humbly to make our requests known to him. We can, and should, ask him to help us. Paul encouraged this type of prayer:

- Ephesians 6:18: Praying at all times in the Spirit, with all prayer and supplication.

- Philippians 4:6: Do not be anxious about anything, but in everything by prayer and supplication with thanksgiving let your requests be made known to God.

- 1 Timothy 2:8: I desire then that in every place the men should pray, lifting holy hands without anger or quarreling.

Everyone should pray about everything all the time is a good motto for our prayer lives. No request is too small, because our prayer life flows out of our relationship with God.

I have prayed about everything all the time in different ways. I make lists, I write on cards, and I put names in my Bible. There is no wrong way to make a prayer request. I think it does help to write it down, though, so we can record God's answer to our prayer. It's good and appropriate to keep praying until we sense God leading us to stop or when he answers clearly. Sometimes I go to God knowing I need to engage his heart on a matter, and I know exactly what my requests are. Other times, I have no idea what to pray. God has given us a promise in Romans 8 to cling to especially in those times:

> The Spirit helps us in our weakness. For we do not know what to pray for as we ought, but the Spirit himself intercedes for us with groanings too deep for words. And he who searches hearts knows what is the mind of the Spirit, because the Spirit intercedes for the saints according to the

will of God. And we know that for those who love God all things work together for good, for those who are called according to his purpose. For those whom he foreknew he also predestined to be conformed to the image of his Son, in order that he might be the firstborn among many brothers. And those whom he predestined he also called, and those whom he called he also justified, and those whom he justified he also glorified (Romans 8:26-30).

Ultimately, we know Jesus is praying perfectly on our behalf. When we don't know what to say, he says it for us. And we have this confidence that his Father bends down to listen.

Andrew Murray said this of prayer:

Though in its beginnings prayer is so simple that the feeblest child can pray, it is at the same time the highest and holiest work to which man can rise. Prayer is fellowship with the Unseen and Most Holy One. The powers of the eternal world have been placed at prayer's disposal. It is the very essence of true religion and the channel of all blessings. It is the secret power and life not only for ourselves, but for others, for the Church, and for the world. It is in prayer that God has given the right to take hold of Him and His strength. It is on prayer that the promises wait for their fulfillment, the Kingdom waits for its coming, and the glory of God waits for its full revelation.[15]

Prayer isn't complicated—not really. But that doesn't mean it's easy. So perhaps it does take a measure of grit to persevere here. I'm still a work in progress, because my walk with Jesus is as well. I want to be that girl who keeps running the race of faith and has a continual conversation with Jesus—who is running ahead of me, behind me, and with me. He is the easiest to talk to because he understands my heart. But I need to remember prayer is so much more than a list of things I need and want. It is, as Murray said, God extending his hand to me and letting me take hold of his strength. It's a channel for his blessings. It's true fellowship with the captain of my salvation.

It's a holy work I get to join.

Oh, that I would do it.

Oh, that we all would.

BIBLE STUDY

Encouragement

Ephesians 1:15-23; Ephesians 3:14-21

Connection

1. Share one statement from the chapter that was most significant to you and why.

2. What makes you get on your knees to pray?

3. Has there been a time in your life when you knew the prayers of a friend or family member made a difference in your life or in the life of someone you knew?

Growth

1. Memorize Ephesians 6:18 (esv): [Pray] at all times in the Spirit, with all prayer and supplication. To that end, keep alert with all perseverance, making supplication for all the saints.

2. Make a plan to intentionally join the conversation of prayer. Perhaps you'll write down the WITH prayer model and work through it once a day. Or ask a friend to keep you accountable.

My Notes:

_____

_____

Walk Worthy

We sit forever in Christ that we may walk continuously before men.

WATCHMAN NEE[1]

Key Scriptures: Ephesians 4:1-2,17-32;
Ephesians 5; Acts 20:32

My house smells like freshly baked bread. You should know this is not a usual occurrence. I mostly gave up the goodness of bread a year or so ago. I say *mostly* because bread is my favorite. I can't forsake it entirely. Especially in times of crisis, I turn to bread.

Today calls for not one but two loaves because a hurricane is headed our way. I've also made brownies, Rice Krispie treats, and muffins. Storms of biblical proportion turn me into Martha Stewart for the good of my family. They are grateful, I assure you.

Over the past few days I've finished all the necessary preparations. I've faced bare grocery store shelves, waited in gas station lines, and resorted to bottling my own water in old soda bottles. I've brought in the porch furniture and watched the Weather Channel app on my phone until my head started to spin just about as fast as the approaching hurricane. Right now it's on its way to devour not simply my town, but the entire state of Florida.

The trouble is it's been coming for days, and we're tired of all the waiting. Today the rain is finally falling faster, and the wind is picking up. There is no avoiding the storm at this point. We have a solid chance we'll lose power for days, and that is truly one of the hardest parts of the unknown. We do what we can to prepare, but then we must walk through whatever comes our way. But don't worry: We will have bread. (Sadly, the brownies are already long gone.)

As I've been making countless hurricane preparations this week, I've also been thinking about what it means for us to walk through life in a different way. All my poetical and pretty introductions have fallen away as I've been doing the very real work of getting my family of six ready for the largest storm to hit Florida in history. As I've prayed about words to land in this book, all I could think about was the storm.

Storms have a way of interrupting our lives and taking over. I've endured more than a few recently. The storms I've faced over the past couple of years have been both literal and metaphorical—the kind that swirl underneath the surface of my heart unseen. Both have tested me to the core. Jesus warned his disciples they would have troubled times: "I have said these things to you, that in me you may have peace. In the world you will have tribulation. But take heart; I have overcome the world" (John 16:33). Since we are his daughters, we can be sure this message is for us as well.

The truths we have been studying in the book of Ephesians should give us great encouragement. Jesus has overcome, and we are seated with him in the heavenly places. In him, we overcome too. We start from this position of rest, but practically speaking, we must walk daily in a world that is dark and in deep need of hope. We look like Jesus when we do; that is entirely the point.

Start Here

Paul uses the word *walk* in Ephesians eight times. Six of those times come in the second half of the letter as he shifts from "dwelling" in the truth of the gospel to "doing" and letting it make a difference in how

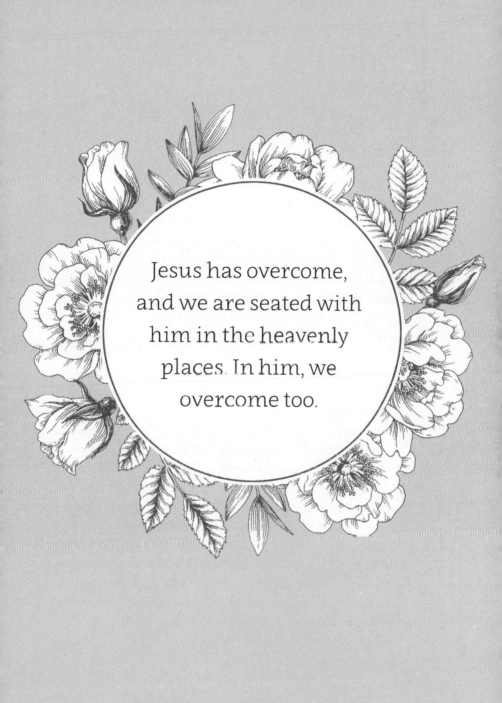

Jesus has overcome,
and we are seated with
him in the heavenly
places. In him, we
overcome too.

we live. He says in Ephesians 4:1, "I therefore, a prisoner for the Lord, urge you to walk in a manner worthy of the calling to which you have been called."

Paul isn't suggesting the Ephesians walk in a manner worthy of their calling; he's pleading with them to do so. The strong emotion he writes with here, after such a beautiful and tender prayer, is like parents calling children close to their side, begging them to do *something*.

I had a talk about the impending hurricane this weekend with my daughters. It sounded like this: "You can be in the house and do your thing during the storm, but if you hear me say, 'Get downstairs!' you best come." Hurricanes can stir up other crazy weather in a heartbeat. This storm was to pass just to the west of our city. This meant we would be on the "dirty side" of the storm—the eastern side. This side is notorious for popping up sudden tornadoes that move quickly and do even more damage than the sustained winds of over 50 mph, toppling trees and sending debris flying. I begged my girls to get to safety if they heard me call for them. I was saying, "Don't delay. Stop what you're doing and come downstairs, away from windows." I wasn't messing around with "If you feel like it" or "When you get around to it." No, with a sense of life-saving urgency, I was beseeching them to listen and heed my call.

Paul had urgency in his voice too. Sitting in a prison cell in Rome, his own personal storm brewing, he didn't have time or the luxury of suggesting they walk in a manner worthy of the grace they had been given. He was urging them to walk in a manner "fitting or suitable"[2] to their calling. It was almost as if he took his pen and drew a big arrow to the beginning of the letter saying, "Remember what you've been called to? Remember who you are in Christ? You are blessed. Chosen. Redeemed. Sealed. Holy and righteous. Walk worthy of that."

Don't mistake Paul's intensity for anger. I think he had parental-like passion flowing through his words. I say something similar to my girls when they go to a school event or to a friend's house. I say, "I love you. Have fun. And remember to act like you belong to somebody." The Ephesians belonged to Jesus. Paul wanted that belonging to drive their behavior.

What did worthy behavior look like? In the next verse Paul says it looks like gentleness, patience, and love (Ephesians 4:2). The foundation of this worthy walk is humility. The Greek word here for "humility" means "a deep sense of one's (moral) littleness, modesty, and lowliness of mind."[3] Consider how monumental this would have been to them:

> The Greeks and the Romans considered humility to be a great weakness, and this kind of attitude was not encouraged or appreciated. Those with meekness were despised and considered worthless. However, this trait was redeemed among believers to represent a distinctively Christlike virtue, which placed the humility of a believer in stark contrast to the high-mindedness of unbelievers who tended to think more highly of themselves than others and even God Himself.[4]

Do you want to have Christlike virtue that stands in contrast to the world? Start with humility. Thank goodness, we don't have to wonder how to do it. Jesus showed us how. Paul said Jesus is our role model for humility in his letter to the church at Philippi:

> Do nothing from selfish ambition or conceit, but in humility count others more significant than yourselves. Let each of you look not only to his own interests, but also to the interests of others. Have this mind among yourselves, which is yours in Christ Jesus, who, though he was in the form of God, did not count equality with God a thing to be grasped, but emptied himself, by taking the form of a servant, being born in the likeness of men. And being found in human form, he humbled himself by becoming obedient to the point of death, even death on a cross (Philippians 2:3-8).

Jesus modeled humility when he emptied himself, taking the form of a servant. He didn't think highly of himself—though he had the right to. His humility led him to pour out his life for others. The world didn't congratulate him. They killed him.

Some things never change. Humility isn't prized today any more than it was two thousand years ago. What is prized is anything and everything associated with self. Don't expect applause when you walk in humility.

As my friend Brooke McGlothlin wrote in her book *Gospel-Centered Mom,* even Christians are sometimes deceived with a "ME gospel," thinking life is all about them instead of the true gospel. The true gospel is marked by humility and thinking of others as more significant than we are (Philippians 2:3). The ME gospel sounds good because it says, "I'm enough. I deserve to be the center of attention." The world likes it. But that isn't what Jesus taught us. "At its core the ME gospel persuades us to worship ourselves instead of God, to believe God exists for us instead of us for Him. Anything that makes much of us while diminishing God is the ME gospel."[5]

Our humility is sourced in Christ. It is completely contrary to the world and our own sinful nature. Paul is calling the Ephesians, and us as well, to a gospel-fashioned life.

He never said it would be easy. We must quit expecting it to be.

Don't and Do

Have you ever been overwhelmed to the point where you just want someone to tell you what to do next? I certainly have felt that way recently. Storms have a way of bringing me to decision fatigue quickly.

I found this to be true to the greatest degree when my husband was in the hospital. I could not make a decision to save my life. In one moment I was standing in a circle of friends trying to decide how to take care of my children. I needed to be on one side of town near my husband, and they were on the other side of town. Fog permeated my every thought. I had no idea how long I stood in that place until someone said, "Stacey, what are you going to do?" I was shaken out of the fog, and I made a call to send a dear girlfriend to stay with the kids. Sometimes it takes plain words and a prompting from others to move forward and do the next thing. That was true over and over for me in the months ahead as Mike recovered.

The Ephesians were in their own storm. They were young believers in a city dark with sin. The corruption around them was overwhelming and tried to permeate every part of their lives. Paul had been nearly killed a couple of years earlier, saved from an angry mob of profiteers enraged over this band of believers. They blamed them (and ultimately Paul) for the downturn in their business built around the goddess Artemis. She ruled the region, and they had no tolerance for Christ followers who didn't support their perverted livelihood.

Paul wanted the Ephesians to know exactly how they were to live in this culture. Their old way of life was no longer an option. He didn't want them to have any questions. Having laid the foundation of humility, he detailed a rather extensive list for what maturity and morality look like in the lives of those who are in the process of becoming like Christ.

Don't: (Old Way of Life)

- be like children (4:14)
- be tossed about with every new wave of teaching by those who want to deceive you (4:14)
- live like Gentile outsiders "devoted to worthless pursuits" (4:17 THE VOICE)
- sin in your anger, giving the devil an opportunity (4:27)
- steal or let corrupt words come out of your mouth (4:28-29)
- grieve the Holy Spirit within you (4:30)
- be bitter, angry, slanderous, or malicious (4:31)
- be sexually immoral or impure (5:3)
- "swear or spurt nonsense" (5:4 THE VOICE)
- be partners with "sons of disobedience" (5:6-7)
- have anything to do with fruitless works of darkness (5:11)
- be foolish (5:17)
- get drunk on wine (5:18)

Do: (New Way of Life)

- speak the truth in love (4:15)

- grow up in every way in Christ (4:15)

- "be renewed in the spirit of your mind" (4:23)

- put on the new self, created in the likeness of God, which is righteous and holy (4:24)

- do honest work and share with those in need (4:28)

- give words of grace to others (4:29)

- "be kind and compassionate" (4:32 THE VOICE)

- forgive each other just as God has forgiven you in Christ Jesus (4:32)

- imitate God (5:1)

- walk in love (5:2)

- walk as children of light (5:8)

- expose the darkness (5:14)

- walk in wisdom (5:15)

- figure out what pleases the Lord (5:17)

- be filled with the Spirit, which causes you to spill out soulful words for others and thankful words to God (5:18-20)

- "submit humbly to one another out of respect for the Anointed" (5:21 THE VOICE)

Over and over, Paul was telling his friends, "We can't depart from the world because we have a responsibility to witness to it; but we must walk in purity and not allow the world to defile us…The Christian life must be radically different from the old life."[6] He even goes into more specifics on how this new way of life plays out in typical relationships like marriage, between children and parents, and between bond-servants and masters. Every believer—no matter what age and stage in life they were in—had a new way of life. Part of this new way of life meant turning from the old. In a place like Ephesus, there would have been daily reminders of who they once were. I'm sure temptation to submit to the overwhelming feeling of darkness was around every corner. Paul was reminding them that a worthy walk looks like Jesus and is different—and, yes, radical.

My friend Angie went on the trip of a lifetime a couple of years ago. She went on a tour of the journeys of Paul, and one stop was in Ephesus. One of the most fascinating stories she shared with me was that early Christians there were baptized in a unique way. They would start out facing the Temple of Artemis. This Wonder of the World was an enormous structure filled with all sorts of pagan worship dedicated to Artemis, the goddess of sex. It glorified the fact that the moral center of the city was totally different from the life of a Christ follower.

Before baptism, the new believer would say to God and all who were gathered, "I renounce Satan and the demons of this world," and then turn away from the temple and step into the water to be baptized.

After they were immersed, they would come out the other side of the baptismal with their backs symbolically toward the temple. The old way of life was behind them. They were demonstrating Ephesians 4:23-24 by taking on what The Message calls "an entirely new way of life—a God-fashioned life, a life renewed from the inside and working itself into your conduct as God accurately reproduces his character in you."

What a beautiful picture this serves for us as we think about the God-fashioned life we live today. Do we need to turn away from something? Is there a way we can do that tangibly in our own lives, showing God our old way of life no longer has a hold on us? God is able and desires to reproduce his life in us. What a gift we've been given.

But how does he do that? Oh, I'm so glad you asked.

Imitate God

At the beginning of chapter 5, somewhat in the middle of the long list of do's and don'ts, Paul gives us a tiny clue when he says, "Be imitators of God, as beloved children" (verse 1). This is a significant statement, because it's the only time in any of his letters Paul says for us to "imitate God." When he wrote letters to the Corinthians, Philippians, and Thessalonians, he placed himself as the example to follow as he, himself, followed and imitated Christ. But not here. He wants the Ephesians to follow God and become like him.

Does this bring a nervous smile to your face, or is it just me? I want to raise my hand and say, "Hey, Paul? Yeah, that's great. But how in the world am I supposed to imitate God? I mean, *he's God*. And last time I looked in the mirror, I was a weary wreck of a girl who needed at least three (okay, four) cups of coffee to get through my day. How does a girl like me imitate a holy, perfect, God?"

This seems like too monumental a task for me, so thank goodness, I'm not alone. I find some comfort in this insight from Tony Merida: "Of course, we cannot imitate God in everything. For example, we cannot create the world of nothing, and we cannot know all things. But we can reflect God's character in some ways as His image bearers who have been changed by the gospel."[7]

Have you been changed by the gospel? Are you being changed by it? Do you know that you bear God's image as you go throughout your everyday life? Paul isn't calling us to an impossible standard and leaving us to throw our hands up into the air and say, "Nope, I can't do that. It's too hard." He's holding up God as an example, and as God's dearly loved children, we are to reflect his character so others will know we belong to him. But he doesn't leave us helpless. He gives us what we need and the power to do it.

If you'll put a marker in Ephesians chapter 5 and turn back with me to Acts 20:32, you'll discover that Paul has already laid this foundation for God's character being found in the lives of his children: "I commend you to God and to the word of his grace, which is able to build you up and to give you the inheritance among all those who are sanctified."

Paul entrusted the Ephesians to God's Word, which was able to build and supply them with everything they would need. God's Word was their spiritual food, and it would equip them to walk out their salvation together. He put them in God's hands, because God was not only committed to the work of setting them apart for his purpose, but to completing the work he began in them and making them like himself.

Turn back to Ephesians chapter 5. (I know we're going a bit back and forth, but I hope you'll stick with me, because we're going to see a beautiful connection. I love that Paul repeats themes and words throughout his letters. It helps me remember so much better.) Look at Ephesians 5:25-27, emphasis mine:

> Husbands, love your wives, as Christ loved the church and gave himself up for her, that he might *sanctify* her, having cleansed her by the washing of water with the word, so that he might present the church to himself in splendor, without spot or wrinkle or any such thing, that she might be holy and without blemish.

I know this part of the passage is talking to husbands, and you are most definitely not a husband. But look with me at what Christ does for his bride and how he does it:

- He loved her.
- He gave himself up for her.

That he might

- sanctify her,
- having cleansed her by the washing of water with the word.

So that he might present the church to himself

- in splendor,
- without spot or wrinkle, or any such thing,
- that she might be holy and without blemish.

The way God cleanses us, purifies us, and frees us from the guilt of sin is through his powerful Word. This is why Paul entrusted his friends to it when he left them. He knew how useful it was. Later he tells Timothy, "All Scripture is breathed out by God and profitable for teaching, for reproof, for correction, and for training in righteousness, that the man of God may be complete, equipped for every good work" (2 Timothy 3:16-17). Paul was continually pointing the Ephesians to the Word of God. And in some of his last words to his beloved son in the faith, he made sure Timothy knew he could lean fully on the Word of God. It would not return void but accomplish a great work in his life (Isaiah 55:11).

> The longer I walk with the Lord,
> the more I need his Word in my life.

The longer I walk with the Lord, the more I need his Word in my life. I don't need it less. I haven't arrived or learned all I need to know. I need to search the Scriptures and find Christ within the pages every day. I can't rest on what I knew yesterday. It's a full-time job to learn to take God at his word and live like I am his daughter. I'm not going to stop needing him for even one moment.

Now, does the busyness of life press me hard some days, and I don't open his Word? Absolutely. I promise you those days are on my calendar as well. But my heart aches when I miss my time with him. I get rough around the edges—quickly. I hear the tone in my voice harshen more quickly when my children push my buttons. (Yes, that happens at my house too.) I fight waves of discouragement thicker when my time with Jesus is pushed aside. I unravel when I am not renewed and revived by his Word daily. To become like God, I require his Word working on my heart continually.

I am so grateful God gave us his words in black and white. I think he knew we would need to see it and hold it in our hands. I don't think he minds at all when we mark up his Word with colored pens or draw pictures in the margins that help us remember it. I think he loves it when we add Bible apps to our smartphones so we always have his Word at our fingertips. He wants us to linger on the page (or screen)

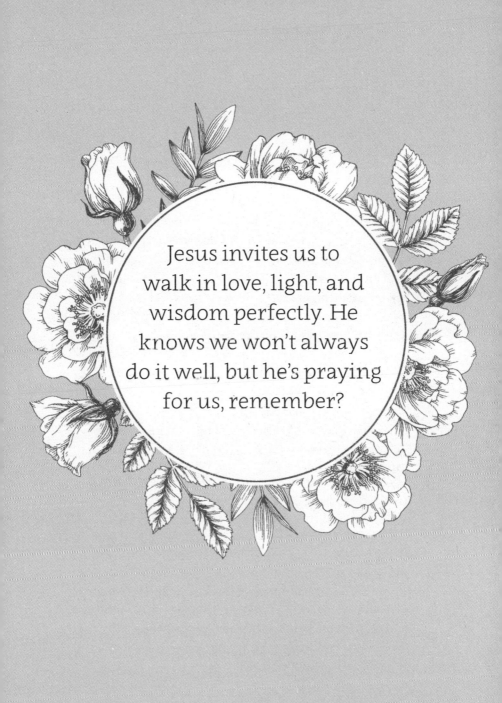

Jesus invites us to walk in love, light, and wisdom perfectly. He knows we won't always do it well, but he's praying for us, remember?

for as long as it takes for it to work its way into our lives. When we do, it doesn't mean we are less like Jesus. It probably means we are looking more like him every day.

In my last book—the first book in the Girlfriends' Guide to the Bible series, on Hebrews and titled *Is Jesus Worth It?*—I wrote a chapter titled "The Word." I prayed and prayed about that chapter, because the Bible might be my favorite thing to talk to women about. In the midst of writing it, God gave me an idea to develop an acronym for how to study his Word. I wanted to make sure you could dig into God's Word on your own. You don't need a seminary degree or tons of big, thick books sitting on your shelf. You can read and understand God's Word because he has given his Spirit within us to teach us and help us understand it. You can sit down with an open Bible, pen, and paper, and study it on your own.

I'm tucking that chapter from *Is Jesus Worth It?* in the back of this book for you to read now or later. It contains the LIFE Bible Study Method and a few words on one of my favorite— and one of the most visually beautiful—verses in the Bible: Hebrews 4:12. (You can also view the LIFE Bible Study Method at a Glance in the back of this book.)

God not only gives us his Word to equip us to live like him; he also gives us the power that enables us. Look at the verses just above the discussion on how Christ washes us with the Word. Paul said,

> Look carefully then how you walk, not as unwise but as wise, making the best use of the time, because the days are evil. Therefore do not be foolish, but understand what the will of the Lord is. And do not get drunk with wine, for that is debauchery, but be filled with the Spirit, addressing one another in psalms and hymns and spiritual songs, singing and making melody to the Lord with your heart, giving thanks always and for everything to God the Father in the name of our Lord Jesus Christ, submitting to one another out of reverence for Christ (Ephesians 5:15-21).

God wants us to be filled and empowered by the Spirit. Paul drew a connection between the Spirit of God and the Word of God. He knew that when we looked at the list of all the do's and don'ts, we would get frustrated. But we *don't* have to do it on our own. God uses his Word to transform us from the inside out. At the same time, the Spirit within us expresses the life of God through us. In humility we submit to this work, and in the process, we reflect that image to the world around us. At least that's what happens when we walk like Jesus. He showed us to walk in love, light, and wisdom perfectly. He invites us to do the same with such grace. He knows we won't always do it well, but he's praying for us, remember? Take encouragement from that. I know I do.

When we walk in a way that brings glory to God, it's a sight to behold. We can't help but burst into worship. We encourage our people with holy words, we thank God for them (whether or not they thank God for us), and we joyfully take on the tasks of the day out of our love and respect for Jesus. How could we not? He has done all the work, and we get to join him.

Oh, friend, that we have the hope of walking worthy and imitating God is a true gift. I want to live to please him. I think you do too, because you are still sitting here in this hard chapter with me. We are called to a high calling. Sometimes it hurts because we feel the weight of that calling in the middle of a storm-ridden life, walking in a broken world that's desperate for Jesus. Just as he did with the Ephesians, God wants us to look like him, live in his love, light the darkness, and live to please him. We don't have a chance on our own. It's only because of his Spirit within us that we can fulfill his will for us to be like him. Only he can awaken us to the truth of his Word and power of his Spirit.

Maybe this would be a good time to tell him what's on our hearts. I'll go first. Feel free to borrow my words or write a few of your own in the space provided at the end of the chapter. He knows our hearts, but it is so good for us to tell him.

Jesus, light of the world; worthy, anointed and liberating king;
perfectly humble servant, I come before you now in awe of you.
You have chosen and redeemed me.
You call me your beloved daughter.
In you, I am sealed with your Spirit.
Through your Word, and by that Spirit,
I ask you to awaken me.
Lord, awaken me.
Awaken in me a desire to humbly and purposefully walk worthy.
Your Spirit desires to please you. Your Word sanctifies me.
Let it be so.
And when I grumble,
when I let fear grow bigger than your character,
and love is the furthest thing from my mind,
when darkness seems to be winning,
and my life looks less like you in any way,
awaken me, Lord, out of my sleep.
Daniel 2:22 tells me, you reveal deep and hidden things.
You know what is in the darkness.
The light dwells in you.
Awaken me to worship you.
Worship sets my heart ablaze with your Spirit.
Worship proclaims my trust of you.
Worship stirs my love for you and others.
Worship pushes back the darkness, which you defeated on the cross.
Worship is gratitude in song.
Awaken me, Lord.
And I will arise.
Christ will shine upon me (Ephesians 5:14).
Let it be so.

BIBLE STUDY

Encouragement

Ephesians 4:1-2

Connection

1. Share one statement from the chapter that was most significant to you and why.

2. Why do you think walking worthy of our calling is so difficult?

3. What do we have working in our favor as we're walking worthy of our calling day in and day out? What has God already provided?

Growth

1. Memorize Ephesians 5:1-2 (esv)—Be imitators of God, as beloved children. And walk in love, as Christ loved us and gave himself up for us, a fragrant offering and sacrifice to God.

2. Paul entrusted the Ephesians to God and his Word of grace to build them up. How will you make sure you're entrusting your own heart to his Word every day? How is God building you up daily in his Word of grace?

My Notes:

_____

_____

_____

_____

_____

_____

_____

In the Trenches

Because this is war. The fight of your life.

PRISCILLA SHIRER[1]

It didn't look like boot camp. It looked like Bible study. Every Sunday night during the summer of 2016, a few girlfriends and I gathered at my friend Angie's house. She always made us dinner, and my friend Erin would bring my favorite coffee to drink while we ate dessert and discussed our study for the week.

Have I mentioned this is truly one of my favorite things to do? Studying God's Word with a group of girlfriends is the best, I tell you. I looked forward to our time together each week. We laughed, we cried, we prayed, we worshiped, and we studied the armor of God. Sitting in the cozy living room together, not one of us thought much about what was going to happen in our lives in the months ahead. We were just grateful to be together. We were hiding God's Word in our hearts.

We didn't know it at the time, but God was making sure we were battle-ready. And, boy, would we need it. I can still see us seated shoulder to shoulder, digging into Ephesians chapter 6 and marveling at God's truth. I saw women eager to know God. God saw warriors who would need every piece of armor we were learning we already had. Thank goodness, we saw only a small part of our story. I think if any of us had had an idea of what was ahead, we might have run the other way. God in his wisdom didn't lead with the battle plan. He led with his truth and relationship. In the midst of Bible study, we got both.

As Paul penned the letter to the Ephesians, he too led with truth and relationship. Looking back, we see the tenderness of his message drawing his dear friends into their relationship with God first. He reminded them they had true worth because of Jesus and his grace that made them part of his holy family. They belonged to him and had a purpose to love and serve him with their lives. He prayed bold prayers over them, demonstrating they could join that heavenly conversation already happening. Out of this beautiful relationship he exhorted them to walk in a manner worthy of all they had been called to. They were alive in Christ. Imitating God was the goal, but they were not alone. He equipped and empowered them to do everything he asked of them.

Paul also knew the Ephesians needed to be battle-ready. He wasn't about to leave out this detail. If the Ephesians were faithful to do all that he had already mentioned, they would most certainly draw the attention of the Enemy. He was certain they would come under fire. The apostle Paul wanted them to know they were not alone. And that they were already victorious.

This is the calling on our lives as well, my friend. As much as I might want to, I can't leave out this chapter.

It isn't that I don't believe the words written here. I cherish these truths. But I need to confess that I'm a bit battle-weary. My time on the front lines has been fierce. If God wants to bring in a soldier to demonstrate swashbuckling, sword-wielding expertise, he most definitely has the wrong girl.

But perhaps he isn't asking me to be perfect. Maybe he's sweetly reminding me of where I've been, and that not once have I walked alone. It's possible that he has brought me to this place to bring encouragement to my heart as well. Wouldn't that be like him?

> When you walk worthy with Jesus,
> your enemy will notice.

Oh, my friend, you need to know that as I study God's Word and write words, I don't have all this figured out. I'm as much in need of these truths as you are. I'm talking to you, but I'm also talking to me. God's Word breathes life into my heart, and I stand in need of it constantly. I don't write books or blog posts or speak at conferences because I've achieved some magical level of spiritual maturity. I do them because God chooses to use the weak things of this world to confound the strong and wise. I promise you, I'm on my knees today, begging him to provide the words we both need.

The bottom line sounds overwhelming, but it's no less true for us than it was for the Ephesians. When we walk worthy with Jesus, the Enemy will notice. We don't have to be afraid of that. We just need to be aware of it. The battle is raging, but we don't have to be taken out by it. We have a calling to stand strong and know whose we are. We have divine protection. We don't have to create it or wish for it. Just like he did for my girlfriends that summer, he is preparing us. He is already at work.

Are you ready? Maybe we could pause right now, right here, and whisper a prayer for one another. You've probably noticed we've done this frequently as we've journeyed through the book of Ephesians. I think it's fitting, don't you? I think Paul would approve. We know that Jesus is already praying for us. Let's join him. I'm praying over you. Take as much time as you need, and then let's move forward together.

> *Lord, the battle is real. The struggle to be effective and not be swallowed up by fear is real. But we have this confidence in you. You have clothed us. You have not left us defenseless. On the contrary, we are victorious already. We have protection. We have weapons that go on the offensive. Lord, teach us. We are listening. I pray your daughters are battle-ready today as we look to you. Remind us you are already in the fight on our behalf.*

Know from Where Your Strength Comes

Paul has preached and pleaded and prayed. His final words to his beloved brothers and sisters reflect all that he has written. He puts it precisely, in almost a bullet-point, journal fashion, with rapid-fire intensity. He doesn't want them to miss this part. He is saying in essence, "Here is what I want to be fresh in your hearts as I put down my pen. I'm sending my final words to you before I wrap up the scroll. Pay attention, friends, because this is important."

He says,

> Finally, be strong in the Lord and in the strength of his might (Ephesians 6:10).

Paul isn't going to go soft in closing words. He doesn't invite them to consider the possibility of being strong in the Lord. He *commands* them to be so. This will require their full obedience.

If Paul were sitting with them instead of reaching out to them through his letter, he would probably raise his voice. He might grab them by the shoulders. He wouldn't lose eye contact, even if his friends squirmed in their seats. He is giving them more than a suggestion. He is giving them a holy pep talk and sending them into the battle. His charge to them is to be strong in the Lord.

So much is in this one statement that I could probably write an entire book on what it is to be strong in the Lord. But let's simply look at the original Greek language here. I say "simply" with a slight smile because there is nothing simple about the Greek language. It's layered with meaning and beauty. The word Paul uses is *endynamoo*, which I think you probably guessed means to be strong.[2] But let's dig a little deeper. More importantly, we need to draw on the other facets of the Greek. Greek verbs have a tense, a voice, and a mood that reveal the true meaning of the words used. This word uses...

- Present Tense: This is happening "now," in the present.
- Passive Voice: The subject (you, the Ephesians, us, and so on) is the recipient of the action (here, to be strong).

Girl, you are not
the strong. Jesus is.

- Imperative Mood: This is an absolute command (not a
  suggestion).

What does this mean? It means we are receiving this strength from
the Lord right now. His strength is acting on you. I am not the strong
one. He is. I find this wonderfully freeing, don't you? Girl, you are not
the strong. Jesus is.

Let's play with that word a little bit more. Paul uses the same word
endynamoo to describe the life of one of my favorite people in the Old
Testament, Abraham. In Romans chapter 4, Paul writes of him, "No
unbelief made him waver concerning the promise of God, but he *grew
strong* in his faith as he gave glory to God, fully convinced that God
was able to do what he had promised" (verses 20-21, emphasis mine).

You might know that Abraham was called the father of Israel. But
he was also a former idol worshiper who followed God imperfectly. He
didn't have it all together. What he demonstrated to us was how to walk
with God being fully convinced that he was able to do what he promised. He grew strong in his faith (by God) as he gave glory to God. The
Message paraphrase reads, "He plunged into the promise and came
up strong, ready for God, sure that God would make good on what
he had said." Don't you love the visual picture there? How was Abraham strong in the Lord? He dove into the promise of God and came
up strong. He didn't let unbelief cause him to stumble.

How are we made strong? We go right back to what we've learned
over and over in the Word of God. Remember God's promises and
what Paul has already said to the Ephesians about strength?

1:19—There is immeasurable great power toward us who believe.

3:16—According to the riches of his glory, he may grant you to be
strengthened with power through his Spirit in your inner being.

We plant ourselves in promise and come up strong.
When we stand here, we don't stagger or stumble.

We can't possibly measure the great power available to us when we don't waver in our belief. God grants us power according to his riches (not ours) through his Spirit. We plant ourselves in promise and we come up strong. When we stand here, we don't stagger or stumble. The command from Paul includes this idea as well: "Do not look in the wrong place for strength. Our strength is not in our resources and ability, on how long we have been Christians, in how much we know about the Bible, or in how long we have been in ministry. Our strength is in our union with Jesus Christ, and his mighty power."[3] If anyone had the right to stand in his own strength, it was Paul. He had a list of credentials he could surely stand on, right? But later, in his other two letters to Timothy, he makes it clear where his strength comes from:

> I thank him who has given me strength, Christ Jesus our Lord, because he judged me faithful, appointing me to his service (1 Timothy 1:12).

> The Lord stood by me and strengthened me, so that through me the message might be fully proclaimed and all the Gentiles might hear it. So I was rescued from the lion's mouth (2 Timothy 4:17).

Paul, like Abraham, knew his strength was solely based on Jesus. He was strong and strengthened in Christ.

So are we. The battle we face requires it. Our puny strength won't do. My friend Lisa Whittle calls it "Jesus Strong" in her book *Put Your Warrior Boots On*.[4] I love how that rolls off the tongue don't you? It's the only strength we can depend on. It's all we need. I don't know what you're facing today. I don't know what you need strength for. But know that, in Christ, you have it, my sister. You are "Jesus Strong." Amen.

Know Whose Armor You Wear

I've been a Christian since I was nine years old. My mom taught me all the Bible songs when I was a little girl. I said my pledge to the Bible every year at Vacation Bible School. I know every flannelgraph lesson I learned from every Sunday school lesson taught in my little Baptist church in Southern Indiana. But I promise you, in my grown-up Bible study this year, I learned something I didn't know about the armor of God. I found this so wonderfully encouraging. I am not embarrassed at all to tell you I was dumfounded that I hadn't known this. I even said out loud, "How did I not know this?"

Paul said, "Put on the whole *armor of God*, that you may be able to stand against the schemes of the devil" (Ephesians 6:11, emphasis mine). The armor you wear is not *your* armor at all. It's called the armor of God because it's *his* armor. You don't earn the armor. You don't create the armor. It's God's own armor. Guess what. You and I are *already clothed in it* because we are in Christ. Earlier Paul said to the Ephesians, "Put on the new self, created after the likeness of God in true righteousness and holiness" (Ephesians 4:24).

When we become Christians, we put on Christ. In God's eyes our new selves take on his nature because we're clothed—or covered—by him. I like how Tony Merida explains it: "We are to put on Christ, which means...to recognize who we are in Christ and to live consistently in that identity with the spiritual resources that are ours."[5] This armor wasn't Paul's idea. He gleaned it from years of studying Old Testament Scriptures like this one:

> The LORD advances like a warrior;
> he stirs up his zeal like a soldier.
> He shouts, he roars aloud,
> he prevails over His enemies. (Isaiah 42:13 CSB)

We see here that God is a warrior ready for battle against his enemies. What we need to know is that our Messiah wears the armor as well:

> He saw that there was no man,
>   and wondered that there was no one to intercede;
> then his own arm brought him salvation,
>   and his righteousness upheld him.
> He put on righteousness as a breastplate,
>   and a helmet of salvation on his head;
> he put on garments of vengeance for clothing,
>   and wrapped himself in zeal as a cloak (Isaiah 59:16-17).

As his daughters, clothed in Christ and living consistently in that identity, we are already armored up. Aren't you encouraged?

If you hang around with me on Instagram, you might be aware of a feature I do almost every Wednesday called "What I Wore." A fellow blogger, Lindsey Cheney, started it on her blog years ago.[6] I loved seeing what she wore every week, so I joined the fun. When I talk to people at church or bump into them at events, they usually ask me about what I wore on Wednesday. I love talking about what I wore. We always want to know stuff like, "Did you get that top at Target?" and "How much was it?" It's fun girlfriend chatter.

But can I tell you something? This armor we wear in Christ is even more exciting.

"What did you wear last Tuesday, Stacey?"

"Girlfriend, I wore the armor of God."

Because in Christ, I always do. So do you. Mercy. What a beautiful truth.

Know Who Your Opponent Is

We need God's strength and his armor because the enemy we face is real and consumed with his attempts to displace God from this world and destroy anything that belongs to him—especially his children. Paul once cautioned the Ephesians by saying, "Give no opportunity to the devil" (Ephesians 4:27). If we aren't going to give him power or occasion to act in our lives, we need to know who he is and what he does.

The term *devil* (or *diabolos* in the Greek) means "a calumniator, false accuser, slanderer."[7] Paul gives us a little more detail about what this opponent does in Ephesians chapter 6, when he says, "Finally, be strong in the Lord and in the strength of his might. Put on the whole armor of God, *that you may be able to stand against the schemes of the devil. For we do not wrestle against flesh and blood, but against the rulers, against the authorities, against the cosmic powers over this present darkness, against the spiritual forces of evil in the heavenly places*" (6:10-12, emphasis mine). Here are a few things I observe about our enemy from these verses:

- Our opponent schemes against us.
- Our opponent is not flesh and blood.
- Our opponent is ruler of this age of darkness.
- Our opponent wants to wrestle with us, causing us to struggle.
- Our opponent is evil and has spiritual forces of evil who do his work.

I seriously doubt the Ephesians were surprised by this. They lived amid the darkness every day. I think today we are at a far greater risk of ignoring our opponent, thinking our real problem is a person we don't especially get along with or a circumstance we can't control. At the same time our culture has made the devil out to be nothing more than a silly prankster or a vice we can't seem to quit. We say, "Oh, the devil made me do it!" with a wink and a smile, all the while not grasping what is truly at stake. I like what Priscilla Shirer says:

> Your real enemy—the devil—wants you to ignore the spiritual reality behind the physical one. Because as long as you're focused on what you can see with your physical eyes, he can continue to run rampant underneath the surface. The more you disregard him, the more damage he is free to do. The enemy may be invisible, but he is not fictional. He is very real, and very persistent, waging war against us constantly.[8]

> We are at war. Our opponent means business.
> We can't afford to disregard him.

We are at war. Our opponent means business. We can't afford to disregard him. Paul said to the Corinthians—and I believe it applies here as well—that we don't want to be outwitted by Satan or ignorant of his designs (2 Corinthians 2:11). Just what are his schemes and designs? Any enemy worth his weight is going to do a couple of things.

First, he's going to try to hinder our growth. The devil doesn't want us moving on to maturity. He especially doesn't want us imitating God in any way, shape, or form. He wants us to remain ignorant of who we are in Christ. He will do everything he can to distract us from the truth of being God's daughter. He doesn't want us to consider Jesus and everything it means to be alive in him. Can you see why the truth we've studied in Ephesians is so important? The devil wants us to be children in our faith and easily tossed back and forth by his lies and our fears. You can be sure that, at the same time, he'll target your potential and keep you from having any influence for Christ. So it's wise for us to be watchful. Our Enemy, Peter reminds us, roams like a roaring lion waiting for someone to devour (1 Peter 5:8). Don't be an easy target.

Second, the Enemy will seek to gain ground in areas where we still struggle. Paul has already mentioned a few of things—like anger, stealing, and harsh words—as potential places we might wrestle with our enemy. I assure you he knows who we once were, and he has a strategic plan to trip us up in these areas. He wants areas of weakness to disqualify us. The ironic thing is our area of greatest potential for influence and places where we struggle are often related.

Let me tell you how this usually shows up in my life. When I wrote my book *Fresh Out of Amazing*, I shared five ways we find ourselves overwhelmed with life. In interviewing women, I'd seen these areas clearly were the top struggles for women like me. They were so like me that I had experienced them all. I'm an overachiever like that.

Now, I like to write from a place of authenticity, but I didn't realize as I wrote each chapter I would experience the same struggles in these areas tenfold. Though I had gained some ground over the years in overcoming my busyness, in comparing myself to others, in believing lies, in healing from heartbreak, and in overcoming grief, I certainly wasn't completely on the other side of victory in most of them. The Enemy exploited this and went on the warpath in my mind. He told me I didn't have any business writing about these things. He said I wasn't qualified to tell women how to walk with Jesus in these areas because I was still in process. He also had the audacity to make me so busy for weeks that I didn't have time to write.

Many times, when I sat down to pour out words on the page, the voice I heard screaming in my ears was that of my scheming opponent, not the whisper of my rescuer. I'm ashamed to admit it, truly, but I almost quit writing that book because I let my fear of failure dominate my thoughts. But slowly, and sweetly, Jesus kept pressing into my heart the truth that he wasn't asking me to be the amazing one. He already had that covered. Jesus also reminded me that his work on my areas of weakness wouldn't be complete until the day I see him face-to-face. Paul echoed this in his letter to the Philippians when he said to them, "I am sure of this, that he who began a good work in you will bring it to completion at the day of Jesus Christ" (Philippians 1:6). The point is Jesus knows I'm a work in progress. What he was asking from me was to stand against the schemes of the devil in his strength, not mine.

What I learned when I turned in that manuscript and watched it make its way into the world was that God delights in using our weak places for his glory. Paul wrote in 2 Corinthians 12:9, "He said to me, 'My grace is sufficient for you, for my power is made perfect in weakness.' Therefore, I will boast all the more gladly of my weaknesses, so that the power of Christ may rest upon me." The potential for impact was in letting God be glorified and use me despite the struggles I'd had over the years.

Can I tell you something? I get the sweetest blessing when women tell me they appreciate my honesty in these areas. They ask me if I've been reading their journals or have a secret insight into their thought life. I assure them the reason I know is because I've been there. I understand, and I'm still growing. Satan wanted to paralyze me from using this part of my life. I'm so grateful I didn't fall (completely) for that scheme.

Have you ever watched a wrestling match? Do you remember how close the opponents were during their match? It makes me wonder what that sport's appeal is, honestly. But we do well to keep that imagery in mind, because it gives us context about our wrestling opponent. "It is a close intense battle, filled with manipulation and strategy. The Devil is not firing laser guided missiles from a distance; he is upon us. Jesus told Peter, 'Satan has asked to sift you like wheat. But I have prayed for you that your faith may not fail' (Luke 22:31-32)."[9]

Oh, friends, our opponent is very real, he is upon us, and it takes nothing less than the full armor of God and the strength of his power to stand against his wicked plans. But we don't have to wonder what that looks like. We have a full-blown how-to manual in the following verses.

Know the Armor

Before we look at the armor of God we wear in Jesus's name, we need to pay attention to something Paul said. It's so important that he repeated it three times in four verses. When I repeat myself, my kids know—or at least they should know—I mean business. I don't repeat myself because I like to hear the sound of my own voice. I do it because I want to draw their attention to something vital. It also may be something I want them to do or not do. Here, Paul said over and over to the Ephesians, "Stand." (In all these verses, the emphasis is mine.)

- Put on the whole armor of God, that you may be able to *stand* against the schemes of the devil (verse 11).

- Take up the whole armor of God, that you may be able to *withstand* in the evil day, and having done all, to *stand* firm (verse 13).

- *Stand* therefore, having fastened on the belt of truth, and having put on the breastplate of righteousness (verse 14).

Stand is his directive. Notice what Paul isn't saying at the same time. He isn't saying "defeat," "fight," "win." He says "stand" repeatedly for a reason.

Watchman Nee wrote,

> The Greek verb "stand" with its following preposition "against" in verse 11 really means "hold your ground." There is precious truth hidden in that command of God. It is not a command to invade enemy territory…God has not told us to do this. We are not to march but to stand. The word "stand" implies that the ground disputed by the enemy is

really God's, and therefore ours. We need not struggle to
gain a foothold on it.[10]

The battle is raging, but it has already been won. Victors don't
need to take territory, because they've already won it. God has already
defeated our enemy. But he hasn't slinked away in quiet surrender. The
devil knows his days are numbered, and he is not happy about it. He's
doing all he can to make a fuss, and his greatest hope is to keep us from
standing. He wants to wrestle us down and pin us to the mat—useless.
But Paul said, "hold your ground," and here is what God has provided
to assure you that you can do just that.

I imagine the checklist that follows as a glorious reminder. Your
belt? Your breastplate? Your helmet? Check! You have it. As you remember each piece and its purpose, you will find this battle armament not
only useful but encouraging.

Weapons of Protection

Belt of Truth: "having fastened on the belt of truth" (6:14)

> You don't fasten the belt of truth in the heat
> of the battle. By then it would be too late.

Here's the good news. Paul had been washing the Ephesians with
the water of the Word of truth all along. He was saying with a fatherly
nod, "You've got this," because they had already fastened the belt of
truth tightly around their waists. Do you ever make a to-do list and
add things you've already done so you'll feel better about your day?
Did you wake up? Did you read your Bible? Drink coffee? "Oh, yes! I
did that already!" (There is no shame with all this making your *done*
list, friends.)

Paul wasn't saying, "You better do this." He was saying, "You have
already done it." That certainly is a good thing, because this part of the
armor is absolutely vital. You don't fasten the belt of truth in the heat

of the battle. By then it would be too late. Here's what Priscilla Shirer tells us about a soldier's belt:

> The Roman soldier's belt or girdle served several purposes. One was to add support and strength to his core…But the other purpose was equally important: the belt secured additional pieces of his armor and kept them solidly in place.[11]

The core support we need to stand is based on the truth of God found in the Word of God. It is foundational because every piece of the protective armor is anchored here. Without truth we would have nothing to attach the rest of the armor to. In addition, it's the first piece of armor we have at our disposal because the devil is a liar. Jesus did not mince words when he called him the "father of lies" in John 8:44. He is a "liar, liar, pants on fire," as my little girls would say. The point is, when we know the truth, we will not be deceived. We will stand.

My friend Erin Warren has been studying truth in depth last year, and I've watched her light up with passion as she talks about truth. If I know one thing for sure, it's that Erin has been girding herself daily. It's no coincidence that the battle around her and her family has been fierce. I've been emboldened by her faith as she has stood, absolutely with the belt of truth around her waist. I love the words she shared with our women's ministry this past year:

> As Jesus and the disciples are sharing the Passover meal, Jesus begins to tell the disciples that He is going away. He has already washed their feet, predicted Judas' betrayal and sent him out and predicted Peter's denial (John 13). Then He says, "Let not your hearts be troubled. Believe in God; believe also in me" (John 14:1). Thomas said to Him, "Lord, we do not know where you are going. How can we know the way?" Jesus said to him, "I am the way, and the truth, and the life. No one comes to the Father except through me" (John 14:5-6).
>
> Plain and simple. All the messages Jesus preached, the words He spoke to His disciples, it all boils down to one

simple truth: Jesus is the way. Jesus is the truth. Jesus is the
life. The Greek word for "truth" means "I am he in whom
the truth is summed up and impersonated." I just love that!
All truth is found in Jesus. He is the sum of all truth![12]

Jesus is the sum of all truth. We are already wrapped up in truth,
girded and alive in him. Ready for battle. He has already made certain
of it.

Breastplate of Righteousness: "and having put on the breastplate of
righteousness" (6:14)

The breastplate for a solider in Paul's time was two-sided and critical,
because it covered both his front and back side. It protected his most
vital organs during the heat of the battle both coming and going. Without the breastplate, a soldier would be vulnerable. For a believer, the
breastplate of righteousness is also twofold—positional and practical.

Positional: The righteousness we wear belongs to God first. In Jeremiah
23:6 we read, "In his days Judah will be saved, and Israel will dwell
securely. And this is the name by which he will be called: 'The Lord is
our righteousness.'" His sacred name is righteousness. He wears it as a
breastplate (Isaiah 59:17) for all to see. Only the righteousness of Christ
is acceptable to God. As his daughters, we are placed in his righteousness. Ultimately, it isn't ours. We wear his "rightness" into battle. He is
our protection and our covering.

*Practical: Clothed in his protection, our righteousness also involves
a consistent and daily walk with Christ.* Satan is the accuser, but the
believer who walks in the light will give Satan no opportunity to attack.
Anchored with the truth fixed about our waists, our goal is to practically apply it daily. When we do this, we walk in a manner pleasing to
God, revealing his righteousness within us.

Shoes of the gospel of peace: "and, as shoes for your feet, having put
on the readiness given by the gospel of peace" (6:15)

At first glance this part of the armor seems a bit puzzling to me.
Why in the world would God clothe us in peace as we stand ready for
the battle? It seems contrary to strap on our shoes laced with peace. I

think it makes sense to say "shoes of boldness" instead, don't you? But if we look back through this letter to the Ephesians, Paul has consistently talked about peace.

- Ephesians 1:2—He greeted them with grace and peace.

- Ephesians 2:14—He said Jesus himself is our peace.

- Ephesians 2:15—He said Jesus's sacrifice created peace between two opposing groups.

- Ephesians 2:17—He said Jesus preached peace to those far off and those near.

- Ephesians 4:3—Paul called the Ephesians to keep the unity of the Spirit in the bonds of peace.

The Greek word for "peace" means "the tranquil state of a soul assured of its salvation through Christ, and so fearing nothing from God and content with its earthly lot, of whatsoever sort."[13] The gospel of peace means we have nothing to fear and that we walk in contentment that can be explained only through our relationship with Christ.

He alone is the best example we have for this type of peace-filled, gospel-centered walking. He demonstrated this peace walk perfectly when he took on flesh and blood. He was never in a hurry. He was not anxious. He carried with him an assurance that his Father in heaven was divinely in charge, and he sought to do everything his Father told him to do.

Do you remember what Jesus said to the disciples in the days just before his crucifixion to calm their fears about what was coming? He said, "Peace I leave with you; my peace I give to you. Not as the world gives do I give to you. Let not your hearts be troubled, neither let them be afraid" (John 14:27). He carried this peace with him wherever he went. He left with peace. And the people were amazed. It doesn't surprise me. They were expecting a warrior who would take possession of the kingdom with force. Jesus indeed set the captives free, but he did it in an entirely different way. He set them free for all eternity, and it was marked with peace in every way.

Paul also spoke about peace in his letter to the Philippians (written near the same time he wrote this letter to the Ephesians.). It must have been on his heart. He said to them, "Rejoice in the Lord always; again I will say, rejoice. Let your reasonableness be known to everyone. The Lord is at hand; do not be anxious about anything, but in everything by prayer and supplication with thanksgiving let your requests be made known to God. *And the peace of God, which surpasses all understanding, will guard your hearts and your minds in Christ Jesus"* (Philippians 4:4-7, emphasis mine).

Oh, sweet friend, the invitation in the middle of this wartime readiness pep talk is to walk in the footsteps of Jesus. He is our peace. He will watch over you. It's not the time for anxious thoughts or fear. You walk in peace. And the world will wonder where your shoes came from.

Shield of Faith: "in all circumstances take up the shield of faith, with which you can extinguish all the flaming darts of the evil one" (6:16)

If you're like me, you like to know the bottom line. Study guides in college were my favorite. I want to be prepared. Period. I certainly don't mind one bit when my pastor gives a sermon and sums up his main point in a sticky statement I can write down in the margin of my Bible and circle with my pretty red pen. I have also been known to send his point out on Twitter, because I figure others might want to know too. So when Paul uses the phrase "above all" in the middle of his checklist of the armor of God, I get a little excited. This is important. Don't miss it.

What does Paul draw our attention to over and above everything else? He says, "Don't forget to raise the shield of faith above all else, so you will be able to extinguish flaming spears hurled at you from the wicked one" (verse 16, THE VOICE). Apparently, as we have already buckled our belt of truth, anchored our breastplate of righteousness to it, and strapped on our peace shoes, the Enemy—the wicked one— has been busy. He's been hurling flaming spears of hate and destruction at us. He has not been merciful at all. He is working overtime, and his attacks are relentless. We have one weapon of protection that will quench those flaming missiles he has with our names on it. That weapon is a shield called faith, and we are called—commanded—to raise it up.

The shield Paul wants us to use is not a minuscule round object we can tuck in our purses. No, this shield is going to take some heavy lifting. Shaped like a door, a Roman soldier's shield was oblong and large enough for him to crouch behind or even get underneath during an enemy attack. Soldiers were even known to line up shoulder to shoulder and put their shields together to make a wall of shields that would protect not only them, but their entire regiment. This type of shield was often made of wood, leather, canvas, and metal. The shield we have as daughters of the King is made of faith. And it has the potential to cover us fully.

The faith Paul is speaking of is the word *pistis* in the Greek. It means "belief with the predominate idea of trust (or confidence) whether in God or in Christ, springing from faith in the same."[14] Do you recall what Scripture says about the devil? He's called the accuser. He is the father of lies, remember? Our faith— belief in Christ—is what protects us with shield-like assurance from his attack of unbelief and doubts. So where does that type of faith come from? Paul said, "Faith comes from hearing, and hearing through the word of Christ" (Romans 10:17). Consider this from Chip Ingram:

> You may go through all sorts of doubts and struggles, bombarded with flaming missiles of the enemy. The shield of faith will extinguish them, but faith can only function around the truths you've been taught...your mind needs to be filled with foundational knowledge.[15]

Girlfriend, raise up that shield of faith. Listen to the words of Christ. This is where battle-ready faith comes from. And you are going to need it every single day.

Your faith shield works optimally when your mind is filled with truth. Don't think for a minute your enemy will stop. He doesn't want you to spend time hearing the words of Christ, studying the Word of God. He wants to keep you busy dodging flaming missiles and chasing doubts. He wants to stir up your unbelief and distract you from what is really going on. But above all, girlfriend, raise up that shield of faith. Listen to the words of Christ. This is where battle-ready faith comes from. And you are going to need it every single day.

Helmet of Salvation: "and take the helmet of salvation" (6:17)

The helmet worn in battle fully encircled the soldier's head. Paul said our spiritual helmet is our "salvation." Our Messiah wears it, and so do we. It protects our mind. The final weapon of protection Paul mentions seems almost an afterthought. But I like to see the beautiful connection between all the pieces. In chapter 1 of Ephesians, Paul says, "In him you also, when you heard the word of truth, the gospel of your salvation, and believed in him, were sealed with the promised Holy Spirit" (verse 13).

- We hear the word of truth (belt of truth).
- Truth is the gospel of our salvation.
- We believe (shield of faith).
- We are sealed with the Holy Spirit (our protection—the armor we wear).

We have this hope in our salvation. It is sure. We don't have to doubt it for one minute.

Weapons of Attack

The Sword of the Spirit: "and take...the sword of the Spirit, which is the word of God" (6:17)

Up until this point the armor of God has provided weapons of protection. I love the security his provision is for my heart. He wraps us up in the most amazing way. But the next two weapons mentioned are not simply for our protection. They are the only offensive weapons we have at our disposal. And, girls, we need to know how to use them with great skill.

First, Paul said, we have the sword of the Spirit, which is the Word of God. God has given us the living, active, sharp Word of God. He has placed it in our hands, and we must be women who know how to wield it. We can't be women who, in the midst of the battle, wonder what God says. We need to know his truth. It must be in our hearts and on our minds. It must be on our lips as words of exhortation and promise. Sometimes we need to say it aloud, so our enemy is aware that we know it's strong and true. We need to proclaim it over our sisters and our spouses and our children.

If you and I think we can set aside this weapon, we are flat-out believing a lie. The Enemy would be happy with us if we followed his lead. Look at what Paul said to Timothy in his final letter to him about last days:

> All who desire to live a godly life in Christ Jesus will be persecuted, while evil people and impostors will go on from bad to worse, deceiving and being deceived. But as for you, continue in what you have learned and have firmly believed, knowing from whom you learned it and how from childhood you have been acquainted with the sacred writings, which are able to make you wise for salvation through faith in Christ Jesus. All Scripture is breathed out by God and profitable for teaching, for reproof, for correction, and for training in righteousness, that the man of God may be complete, equipped for every good work (2 Timothy 3:12-17).

> We can't draw our swords if we don't
> know how to use them.

If Timothy was living in the last days, you can be sure we are too. Do you see it? Are you experiencing times of difficulty? Have you noticed people loving themselves lately on Facebook? Those who walk in a manner worthy of their calling will have times of persecution and trials. This is not the time to shrink back. This is the time for us to continue in what we have learned, and to remember that the Word of God will equip us for every good work. This is the heart and passion behind The Girlfriends' Guide to the Bible series. We can't draw our swords if we don't know how to use them. We can't fight with a sword that belongs to our sister. We don't want to be weak women who can't arrive at a knowledge of the truth. We need to grasp the sword of the Spirit by faith, asking God to teach us, reprove us, correct us, and yes, to train us in righteousness.

And the Enemy won't even know what hit him.

Prayer: "pray at all times" (6:18-20)

> [Pray] at all times in the Spirit, with all prayer and supplication. To that end, keep alert with all perseverance, making supplication for all the saints, and also for me, that words may be given to me in opening my mouth boldly to proclaim the mystery of the gospel, for which I am an ambassador in chains, that I may declare it boldly, as I ought to speak (Ephesians 6:18-20).

We've already spent a great deal of time talking about prayer, so I'll say here only that this weapon of attack is what energizes the rest of the armor. It does it by keeping us in constant conversation with our Father. Paul said when we pray at all times, we are alert with perseverance. Prayer is what makes us ready, and Paul said don't stop—essentially, "Pray all the time. With all prayers. With all the perseverance. For all the saints. And while you're at it, pray for me too."

That last part especially tugs at my heart. Do you think Paul was above needing that kind of prayer on his behalf? Do you think your pastor wouldn't be blessed if you said, "Hey, I'm praying for you, and I won't stop"? I know it's easy to think our spiritual leaders are above needing it. But I assure you, if God has placed someone in your life worth imitating as they imitate God, your constant prayer will be a treasure to them.

A Beautiful Picture

I'm sitting here thinking about each of those precious women I went through Bible boot camp with during the summer of 2016. We thought we were doing a good thing. We just didn't know what was ahead, and honestly, I'm glad we didn't have any idea what God was preparing us for. I found those same sisters by my side when my family of six faced the hardest battle of our lives. They were "armored up." They made sure I was too. And when I fell down, couldn't find my footing, and forgot how to use my armor, they surrounded me—shields up. They prayed for me, and they helped me to my feet. More importantly, we weren't in the battle alone. Jesus was with us too.

What a beautiful picture there in the trenches.

BIBLE STUDY

Encouragement

Ephesians 6:1-20

Connection

1. Share one statement from the chapter that was most significant to you and why.

2. What truth from the book of Ephesians have you girded yourself with over the past couple of weeks, acting as a belt of truth for you today?

3. Do you want to sharpen one part of God's armor with deeper study? What part of the armor do you want to understand better?

Growth

1. Memorize Ephesians 6:10-11 (ESV): Finally, be strong in the Lord and in the strength of his might. Put on the whole armor of God, that you may be able to stand against the schemes of the devil.

2. Pray through the armor every day this week to remind yourself what is already available to you as you are clothed in the righteousness of Christ.

My Notes:

_____

_____

_____

_____

_____

_____

_____

Three Ways Not to Lose Your First Love

Define yourself radically as one beloved by God...God's love
for you and his choice of you constitute your worth. Accept
that, and let it become the most important thing in your life.

JOHN EAGAN[1]

Key Scriptures: Ephesians 6:21-24;
Ephesians 5:2; Isaiah 54:10; Revelation 2:1-7

"You have no idea how loved you are."

This was the significant and yet simple statement my pastor spoke softly as we stood in my husband's ICU room. I was wading through a fierce sea of fear, feeling myself getting sucked under another wave when his words cut through. I nearly stumbled when he said it. This didn't surprise me too much, because over and over during those first few days, I had felt knocked off my feet and unable to stand. Every few minutes I was looking for a place to sit down for fear I would crumple onto the cold hospital floor.

But this was a different jarring. It wasn't bad news. It wasn't grim. It was an encouraging word I desperately wanted to grab onto. Yet in the moment I just didn't have a place to file it in my brain. Instead, I think I smiled weakly, nodded, and said, "Thank you," knowing I would need to bring it back out another day when I had a bit more energy to consider it. At the time, I was using what little I had left to do truly important things, like breathing in and out and not falling down.

Sometime later, after my husband woke up and my days were filled with more bedside sitting and more waiting for doctors to come in and out, I thought about what my pastor said. He knew I was in shock and that my margin was small. What he wanted to do, I believe, was draw my attention to what had transpired all around my family during those early days. He wanted me to see the overwhelming love of God, the response of his people, and to find a measure of encouragement. I began to replay many of those moments in my mind. Our friends and church family loved us so well:

- They came rushing to the hospital in the middle of the night.

- They watched my girls.

- They stayed with us.

- They clothed me.

- They fed me.

- They cried with me.

- They prayed bold prayers when all I could do was cry out small words to Jesus.

- They refused to give up hope.

These were the expressions of love I was personally aware of. I know, there must have been so much more happening all around us that I didn't see because my vision was so narrow. Peeling back the layers of this holy disruption has been a slow healing for my family. Over a year has passed, and we are still unwinding it all. But those words voiced to me over the hum and beeps of machines keeping my husband alive were tucked deep in my heart. Even though much of what I remember about those days are clouded, God made sure I remembered this with clarity. I can't tell you how grateful I am for his mercy in reminding me, and for my pastor for saying it.

You have no idea how loved you are.

Those words came back to me recently, but in a different way. Jesus was wrapping his arms around me saying, "Do you see it? Here in my Word, I met you in Ephesians. You found me here. And mostly, what I'm doing here is loving you. Do you have any idea how loved you are?"

The message of this book is as simple as the song we might have learned in preschool—"Jesus loves me this I know, for the Bible tells me so." It is by far the most important thing about us. We are loved more than we know. This truth, when tucked deep inside our hearts, can change us. I think it's what God wants us to know today as we close out this book

Do you have any idea how loved you are?

My prayer is that you will be reminded you are loved. Because, my sweet friend, you are. So loved.

LYLAS

Before I sent my first email in college to a cute guy named Mike, whom I later married, I perfected the art of letter writing to my best girlfriends. We took turns writing our life stories on college-ruled notebook paper and folded them perfectly in tiny shapes we could pass during English class or shove in between the vents of each other's lockers. Nearly every letter I wrote included the closing LYLAS—"love ya like a sister"—because that was what we were— sisters. We were sisters for that season of life. We even had matching T-shirts with our nicknames printed on the backs of them. Since I didn't have any real sisters, I took this relationship seriously.

Paul took his relationship with the Ephesians seriously too. In his closing statement to them, he wrapped up his message, making sure he didn't leave anything out. He might not have used LYLAS, but he chose words with deep meaning:

> Peace be to the brothers, and love with faith, from God the Father and the Lord Jesus Christ. Grace be with all who love our Lord Jesus Christ with love incorruptible (Ephesians 6:23-24).

With his final words of good-bye, Paul reaches back to reflect the beginning of his letter, where he said, "Grace to you and peace from God our Father and the Lord Jesus Christ" (1:2). In between the beginning and ending of the letter, Paul wrote a beautiful story, weaving together the grace and peace of God in the lives of the Ephesians. It was fitting for him to bookend his letter with grace and peace. I'm sure these were at the front of his mind when he thought of blessing his friends. At the same time, Paul's letters typically concluded with blessings of "peace and grace," much like I signed my letters in middle school with LYLAS.

Though his words were heartfelt, I'm sure, it wasn't out of the ordinary for Paul to conclude his letters in this way. I do this as well, when I sign my name or send an email. It might relieve you to know, I don't use LYLAS anymore. However, I typically sign my name the same for personal and most business correspondence. I write, "Looking forward," which is a nod to some of my favorite verses in Hebrews (12:1-3) and a reminder to my own heart to keep looking to Jesus, no matter what.

Paul wanted to remind the Ephesians of something too. He didn't want them to forget a central theme in his letter, and so he added it to his signature blessing of "grace and peace," not once but three times.

- *Love* with faith from God the Father and the Lord Jesus Christ
- All who *love* our Lord Jesus Christ
- With *love* incorruptible

This probably shouldn't come as a surprise to us, because Paul pulls a strong thread of love all the way through the letter, mentioning love at least nine other times. I think he wanted his beloved Ephesians to remember they were deeply tethered to this love. It marked their lives. He also wanted them to grab onto that thread with everything they had. He knew fickle-hearted love would never sustain them. His blessing and simultaneous calling for them was to a fierce love that would not fade away. It would be without corruption. It would not die but grow stronger every single day. He didn't want them to lose their first love.

But how would they do that? How do we?

Remember Your First Love

The love Paul is talking about in his benediction blessing is called "agape" for a reason. It means "affection or good will." But at its core, this kind of love is found only in God. It is "a purely biblical and ecclesiastical word…and noticeable that the word first makes its appearance as a current term in Song of Solomon, frequently used in the writings of Paul most often used in 1 Corinthians—which Paul wrote FROM Ephesus"[2] You might remember that in 1 Corinthians, Paul said this kind of incredible love is from God the Father through Jesus Christ and it never fails (13:8). Remember, Paul has already prayed their roots would run deep in agape. This is where he asked God to ground them. Paul knew they would never find another love that could take its place.

I think Paul was encouraging them to look back even while they were looking forward. I want you to feel the freedom to do that as well. Turn back to Ephesians 2 and let his love woo you right back to the heart of your Father. Your first love passionately pursues you like this:

> God, being rich in mercy, because of the great love with which he loved us…made us alive (Ephesians 2:4-5).

God has loved you with a great love. Other translations say this love is

- unfathomable (THE VOICE), and

- incredible (MSG).

God has great, unfathomable, incredible love, and he has poured it out on us. He has embraced us—the hopelessly outcast ones, if you recall—with this exact kind of love.

Does it soften your own heart to reflect on this? I don't know why we don't grasp how loved we are. Maybe it feels too good to be true because the trials in our lives seem to say otherwise. Or maybe we believe the lie that we're not worth being loved in such a way. Perhaps you are like me. As much as I doubt how loved I am by those around me, I also doubt the love of God at times. Yet this has been the heart of the Father for his children throughout all generations: God has never hidden his love for us. It has never been a secret; it's been on display for all to see:

> "The mountains may depart
>   and the hills be removed,
> but my steadfast love shall not depart from you,
>   and my covenant of peace shall not be removed,"
> says the LORD, who has compassion on you (Isaiah 54:10).

Toward the end of my senior year at Indiana University, I had the chance to take a mission trip to Albania a few months after it fell from the grip of communism. Forty other students and I were some of the first American missionaries inside the country. This remarkable trip radically changed my life.

On our way there, we made a short stop in Zurich, Switzerland, before boarding our last plane to Tirana—the capital of Albania. Exhausted from traveling all night from the States, I quickly dozed. As the sun came up that morning, I felt a gentle hand touch my shoulder. The stranger next to me, who happened to be a pilot from a different airline, made eye contact and said, "You can't sleep through this."

I followed his outstretched hand and gazed out the window to the most unbelievable sight I had ever seen. Miles below, the snow-capped Swiss Alps spread before me, glistening in the early morning light like a handful of diamonds. The sight took my breath away; I had never seen such beauty.

I smiled at my new friend and thanked him. He sat back, pleased that he had made the right decision in waking a tired and clueless college student.

Later that week, I walked onto the campus of the University of Tirana and had the opportunity to share the gospel with students who had never heard the name of Jesus. Three girls in particular stole my heart with their sweet response. They had tears in their eyes as they bowed their head and responded to his steadfast love for them. In three languages (English, Albanian, and broken French), we talked excitedly of that love, and they began a relationship with their Savior that day.

On my way back over the Swiss Alps, once again I was struck by their beauty. This time I didn't need a reminder not to miss them. I was actively looking forward to it with great expectation. They did not disappoint. It's remarkable to me that this is the display of grandeur God chooses to use as a comparison to his incredible love in Isaiah 54:10. His Word reminds us the Alps could crumble to the ground and dissolve into the sea, but God's love will never do that. His love is steadfast. His love never ends. It can't be removed.

I'm so glad I didn't miss witnessing his love in a cold dormitory room in Tirana, Albania, in the spring of 1993. The Alps in all their beauty could not compare to the passionate, pursuing love of Jesus for his three daughters. They didn't miss it either. God sent a weak and weary college girl, who had never traveled out of her own country and didn't speak their language, to touch their shoulders and say, "You don't want to miss this. Jesus loves you and wants to love you forever." Oh, friend, you can't miss it either.

Looking once again at Ephesians 2, we see this grand demonstration of just how much he loves us:

> Even when we were dead in our trespasses, [God] made us alive together with Christ —by grace you have been saved— and raised us up with him and seated us with him in the heavenly places in Christ Jesus, so that in the coming ages he might show the immeasurable riches of his grace in kindness toward us in Christ Jesus (Ephesians 2:5-7).

The demonstration of his great love is the gospel. That love took our place, died on a cross, and saved us. Agape raised us up and seated us with him in the holy place, so that in the ages to come—forever and ever—he could extend that kindness and cherish us perpetually. This love never goes through decay. It can't, because it has already died and been raised up to live forever.

Brennan Manning wrote,

> God created us for union with Himself: This is the original purpose of our lives and God is defined as love (1 John 4:16). Living in awareness of our belovedness is the axis around which the Christian life revolves. Being the beloved is our identity, the core of our existence. It is not merely a lofty thought, an inspiring idea, or one name among many. It is the name by which God knows us and the way He relates to us.[3]

> This is the love we were made for. Let it woo you and win you over and over with the sweetness and the sacrifice.

Beloved girl, God's love for you can't be removed. His love for me will not be restrained. It is agape. And just like my three sisters in Albania experienced, you are his, and he calls *you* by name (Isaiah 43:1). It isn't a fad or a hashtag. This is the love we were made for. Let it woo you and win you over and over with the sweetness and the sacrifice.

Walk in Love

Our first love fuels the love we give back to God. The wooing is wonderful, but the continued calling on our lives is to go deeper and make progress from that beautiful, beloved identity. Ephesians 5 says,

> Watch what God does, and then you do it, like children who learn proper behavior from their parents. Mostly what God does is love you. Keep company with him and learn a life of love. Observe how Christ loved us. His love was

not cautious but extravagant. He didn't love in order to get something from us but to give everything of himself to us. Love like that (5:1-2 MSG).

How do we cultivate incorruptible love? We keep company with the source of it and become like him. Doesn't it encourage you to know you can learn a life of love? Jesus loved without restraint. He poured out every drop, holding nothing back, and he didn't do it to gain anything from us. He gave his life. Period. This is our example:

> Walk in love, as Christ loved us and gave himself up for us,
> a fragrant offering and sacrifice to God (Ephesians 5:2).

Jesus, Lamb of God, was a pleasing sacrifice to God. I doubt seriously that sin offerings in the temple smelled good. But the sacrifice of Jesus was different. It was a "sweetsmelling savour" (KJV) to the Father. It pleased him and satisfied the sin debt we owed. He accepted it with pleasure. When we love like that, we look like him. We even smell like him:

> Thanks be to God, who in Christ always leads us in triumphal procession, and through us spreads the fragrance of the knowledge of him everywhere. *For we are the aroma of Christ* to God among those who are being saved and among those who are perishing, to one a fragrance from death to death, to the other a fragrance from life to life. Who is sufficient for these things? For we are not, like so many, peddlers of God's word, but as men of sincerity, as commissioned by God, in the sight of God we speak in Christ (2 Corinthians 2:14-17, emphasis mine).

Walking in love means we spread the fragrance of the knowledge of Christ everywhere. We speak, and Christ's name hangs in the air like a lovely perfume.

I always think of these verses with a smile and remember my dear friend Lori. A few years ago, during a Bible study we both were part of, we memorized them. Lori had a flair for making gifts, and she gave each of us a tiny bottle of Sweet Pea Body Lotion from Bath & Body Works with verse 15 attached to it. She smiled at each one of us and said, "Girl, you smell good. You smell like Jesus." When we caught one another growing in his love and demonstrating his love to others, we would hug each other and say, "You smell good, girl." Every time I see that lotion, I think of her and the sweet challenge to remember that I can smell like Jesus too.

The same is true for all of us who call on his name. When we walk in a manner worthy of our calling, God spreads his sweet aroma through us. But keep in mind that not everyone will appreciate that fragrance. To those who are being saved, it is life. His love brings life. To the perishing world around us, it's a reminder that, in their rejection of his undying love, they have sentenced themselves to death.

Matthew Henry wrote,

> Unto some it is a savour of death unto death. Those who are willingly ignorant, and willfully obstinate, disrelish the gospel as men dislike an ill savour, and therefore they are blinded and hardened by it: it stirs up their corruptions, and exasperates their spirits. They reject the gospel, to their ruin, even to spiritual and eternal death. Unto others, the gospel is a savour of life unto life. To humble and gracious souls the preaching of the word is most delightful and profitable. As it is sweeter than honey to the taste so it is more grateful than the most precious odours to the senses, and much more profitable; for as it quickened them at first, when they were dead in trespasses and sins, so it makes them more lively, and will end in eternal life.[4]

Humble and gracious souls will find the fragrance of Christ sweeter than honey. The world will not always love the fragrance of Christ we carry with us. But the body of Christ—just like my friend Lori—will savor that sweet, sweet smell, and it will encourage them.

Remember, mostly what God does is love you. May that be what we also do in his name in the lives of others. May we love people like he does and let that hang in the air long after we leave the room.

Pray

This won't come as a surprise to you, I'm sure. Once again, we return to prayer to keep in step with Jesus. Paul prayed the Ephesians would already be rooted in love and understand the height and depth of it. It doesn't surprise me that Paul breathes out the final words of this letter in the form of a prayer, asking that their love would be undying for Jesus. Paul was following the example of Christ. Look what Jesus prayed on the night he went to the cross to make that ultimate sacrifice of love for you and for me:

> Father, I desire that they also, whom you have given me, may be with me where I am, to see my glory that you have given me because *you loved me before the foundation of the world*. O righteous Father, even though the world does not know you, I know you, and these know that you have sent me. I made known to them your name, and I will continue to make it known, *that the love with which you have loved me may be in them, and I in them* (John 17:24-26, emphasis mine).

God loved Jesus with agape love before the foundation of the world. The night of his betrayal, Jesus prayed this same love would be in you and me before he demonstrated his love for us by dying on the cross. Today Jesus is sitting at God's right hand and lives to make intercession for you and me (Hebrews 7:25). I believe his continued prayer is one of agape love over our hearts.

Love like mountains standing tall.
In his embrace you will never fall.

Does this increase your resolve to join him in that prayer? You are loved and prayed for with a love that began before those mountains ever came to be and before the same God spoke light into being. He loved you with agape love. He desires you to not only know it, but to walk in it. This love is never going to end. I believe prayer is part of what keeps our hearts in tune with his. Jesus prayed for it. Paul echoed that prayer. Let us make it our prayer as well.

The Part I Wish I Could Leave Out

If only we could join hands right now, sing a hymn of praise, and go on our merry little way. I feel loved and cherished in the most amazing way, don't you? Well, we'll get to that hymn, I promise. How I wish we could close this book right here. But I wouldn't be able to sleep tonight if I left out this last part.

Have you ever had to tell a friend a hard thing with a strong dose of love? I have. Those conversations have never been my favorite. Still, confrontations come up from time to time, and I always bathe them in prayer. So before you read the next paragraph, please be assured that I'm praying for you. Mercy, I'm praying for all of us.

We've come to the final verse in Ephesians, but we aren't at the end of the Ephesians' story. If you turn to the last book in the Bible, you get a sad little addition to their story and the answer to the question, "What happens when you lose your first love?" Revelation 2 tells us:

> To the angel of the church in Ephesus write: "The words of him who holds the seven stars in his right hand, who walks among the seven golden lampstands. I know your works, your toil and your patient endurance, and how you cannot bear with those who are evil, but have tested those who call themselves apostles and are not, and found them to be false. I know you are enduring patiently and bearing up for my name's sake, and you have not grown weary. But I have this against you, that you have abandoned the love you had at first. Remember therefore from where you have fallen; repent, and do the works you did at first. If not, I will come to you and remove your lampstand from its place, unless you repent. Yet this you have: you hate the works of the Nicolaitans, which I also hate. He who has an ear, let him hear what the Spirit says to the churches. To the one who conquers I will grant to eat of the tree of life, which is in the paradise of God" (Revelation 2:1-7).

Heartbroken? I am. This part of the story makes me want to cry. I feel like I know these people. They are my friends. We've watched Paul pour out his life for them. They have been discipled well. And yet the very thing Paul warned them about has come true. Remember these strong words?

> Pay careful attention to yourselves and to all the flock, in which the Holy Spirit has made you overseers, to care for the church of God, which he obtained with his own blood. I know that after my departure fierce wolves will come in among you, not sparing the flock; and from among your own selves will arise men speaking twisted things, to draw away the disciples after them. Therefore be alert, remembering that for three years I did not cease night or day to admonish every one with tears (Acts 20:28-31).

So what happened? What went wrong?

Well, let's look at the fact that they did some things right. It's always positive to start with the good:

- They worked and had patient endurance.
- They couldn't bear with those who were evil.
- They tested those who called themselves apostles.
- They were enduring patiently.
- They had not grown weary.

All good things, right? It seems to me that the Ephesians excelled at doing and enduring. They were keepers and doers to the core. Guess what. I am too. No wonder I like them so much. What didn't go so well? This: "But I have this against you, that you have abandoned the love you had at first" (Revelation 2:4).

My child, you have left your first love.

And I have this against you.

How did this happen? Is it possible they forgot to remember how they were loved with an undying love? Did they stop keeping company with Jesus? Did they neglect to pray? Did other loves take first place in their hearts?

We don't know for certain. We do know what God wanted them to do promptly. He said, "Remember therefore from where you have fallen; repent, and do the works you did at first. If not, I will come to you and remove your lampstand from its place, unless you repent" (Revelation 2:5). The remedy is clear. Jesus is saying, through the apostle John, "Remember and repent. Turn around. You're going the wrong way. Go back to the beginning and do what you did then. Remember the joy and how much your first love meant to you when you turned your back on the world and responded with all your heart? Go back. Walk with me in that way. Enjoy all that I have set aside for you in your relationship with me. Grab hold of that freedom and live a life worthy of your calling. Walk with me, once again turning from your sin."

But his warning is just as clear: "If you don't remember and repent, I'll come and 'remove your lampstand.' The beautiful city on a hill shining in the darkness will shine no more because I'll remove it. Your influence as the body of Christ will be gone. I'd rather remove my church entirely than let you chase after other loves more than me."

And so here we sit with this gray cloud of warning for our dear friends and a few questions we must answer for ourselves. We can't discard their warning without applying it to our lives. And please know, this keeper and doer is talking to her own heart first.

Do you love God with an undying love?

Is he your first love? Always?

Have you forgotten him?

Have you chased after other loves more than him?

What about during trials and persecution?

Will you love God when fierce wolves *from among you* try to pull you away from truth?

Will you love him even then?

Stand with the woman caught in her sin
and see his grace eyes only for you.

Remember
your first love.
Live out of it.
Live toward it.

Are your tears flowing ugly now too? We can look back at the Ephesians and see a tiny bit (or a great deal) of our hearts as well. It isn't easy to see, I know. Ask God to show you. I mean, really show you where you might have gone astray. Stand with the woman caught in her sin and see his grace eyes only for you. His warning is full of tenderness. But don't let this moment of truth pass you by.

And now wipe those tears away. Once you have turned from that way of living, take heart, my friend. There is good news. And it's better than we could have hoped for. Think about this:

> From hound-dog disciples and sour faced saints, spare us, oh Lord! Frederick Buechner wrote, "Repent and believe in the gospel, Jesus says. Turn around and believe the good news that we are loved is better than we ever dared hope, and that to believe in that good news, to live out of it and toward it, to be in love with that good news, is of all glad things in this world the gladdest thing of all. Amen, and come, Lord Jesus."[5]

It isn't over yet. John gives us this strong dose of tough love that I'm sure Paul would have stamped with approval. Go back to the way you used to love God. Turn your life around and do what you know you should be doing in the first place.

Remember your first love.

Live out of it.

Live toward it.

Be in love with the good news that you are loved.

And, truly, it is better than you or I could have hoped for.

That Hymn I Promised

I think John, in writing this part of Revelation, was reaching back across the years and reminding the Ephesians of the same incorruptible love Paul blessed them with in his benediction. Dear friends, how do we keep from losing our first love?

We remember.

We walk in love.

We pray.

We do the works we did at first (Revelation 2:5). And for those of us who are willing to listen and do these things, Jesus makes this promise: "I will grant to eat of the tree of life, which is in the paradise of God" (2:7).

Do you know what I believe with all my heart? Jesus is for us in the most extraordinary way. We know he prays for us too, remember? But did you know he is singing over us as well? Zephaniah 3:17 says, "The Lord your God is in your midst, a mighty one who will save; he will rejoice over you with gladness; he will quiet you by his love; he will exult over you with loud singing." Your first love is singing over you, beloved girl. If we could lean in to listen, it might sound a little bit like this:

> The love of God is greater far
> Than tongue or pen can ever tell;
> It goes beyond the highest star,
> And reaches to the lowest hell;
> The guilty pair, bowed down with care,
> God gave His Son to win;
> His erring child He reconciled,
> And pardoned from his sin.
>
> Oh, love of God, how rich and pure!
> How measureless and strong!
> It shall forevermore endure—
> The saints' and angels' song.
>
> Could we with ink the ocean fill,
> And were the skies of parchment made,
> Were every stalk on earth a quill,
> And every man a scribe by trade;
> To write the love of God above
> Would drain the ocean dry;
> Nor could the scroll contain the whole,
> Though stretched from sky to sky.[6]

This line gets me every time: "To write the love of God above would drain the ocean dry."

I suppose we could try to understand his perfect, incorruptible love for us, but maybe we never will in this life. It will most likely take eternity for us to grasp the smallest drop.

"You have no idea how loved you are."

Maybe that's the point after all.

Beloved.

Be loved.

Love.

Looking forward,
Stacey

BIBLE STUDY

Encouragement

Revelation 2:1-7

Connection

1. Share one statement from the chapter that was most significant to you and why.

2. Do you struggle with believing you are loved?

3. How does consistently walking in love look to you? What part of the three ways we are challenged not to lose our first love is the most difficult? The easiest? Why?

Growth

1. Memorize Ephesians 6:23-24 (ESV): Peace be to the brothers, and love with faith, from God the Father and the Lord Jesus Christ. Grace be with all who love our Lord Jesus Christ with love incorruptible.

2. Attempt to thank and write the love of God for you in a prayer back to him. Can you do it? This would be a beautiful testimony to share with others.

My Notes:

_____

_____

_____

_____

_____

_____

_____

Start a Girlfriend Group

I've talked with women all over the country, and I believe God is stirring the hearts of his daughters with a hunger for biblical literacy. God has moved in my heart too. The Girlfriends' Guide to the Bible is a series I wish I had when I started studying God's Word years ago. Each book in the series will offer fresh, friendly, and faith-renewing wisdom on specific books of the Bible—perfect for individuals and groups alike.

The first book—*Is Jesus Worth It? Igniting Your Faith When You Feel Like Quitting*—released in September 2017. It's based on the book of Hebrews. The second book is the one you're holding in your hand—*When Grace Walks In: Passionately Pursued, Incredibly Loved*—and it's based on the book of Ephesians.

Along with the series, I have a vision for groups of girlfriends to gather all over the world, around tables, and in living rooms with the Word of God open between them. Imagine, if you will, a small group of women walking through a book of the Bible together. They would meet weekly for 6–8 weeks, study Scripture, read the corresponding Girlfriends' Guide to the Bible book as a companion, and pray together. This group would be rooted in Scripture, be strong in relationship, and allow girlfriends to start biblical conversations about everyday living.

This past year at my home church, we launched Girlfriend Groups and saw over 22 groups form. Women from all ages (ninth-grade girls to women in their seventies), all backgrounds, all stages (single women, married women, moms), all relationships (friends, coworkers, neighbors, professionals), and different languages opened God's Word together in community. The response was amazing, and the feedback we received from women was encouraging. One woman said about her Girlfriend Group,

> The beauty of studying and discussing God's Word showed itself every week as pastors' wives, pastors' daughters, married women, mommas, single women, and women of all ages came together. We simply talked about the truth of who they learned Jesus was and the truth of who Jesus said that we were. We all had one thing in common—we wanted to have women around us to encourage us to stay plugged into the Word.
>
> Every week without fail, someone always shared something that the rest had not seen or caught. Hearing how the Word spoke to each woman and where Jesus met her that week was not only encouraging but comforting. Tears were shed and laughter shared as identities were re-identified and viewpoints of who Jesus is were softened and changed us.
> —*Katie T., Girlfriend Group Leader*

I can't wait for you to get started. I have several resources that might be of interest to you. Find them on my website:

The Guides:

Is Jesus Worth It? (Hebrews)

When Grace Walks In (Ephesians)

Group Information:

http://staceythacker.com/girlfriends-group/

Finally, keep reading to see a sample chapter from *Is Jesus Worth It?* titled "The Word." If you have any questions, don't hesitate to contact me. I'd love to walk alongside you.

The Word

Taken from *Is Jesus Worth It?*

Hebrews 4:12-16; Deuteronomy 32:45-47

I think I speak for most parents and grandparents when I say school presentations are equal parts triumphant and tedious. The triumphant parts include our own tiny people who have worked hard on their lines and songs. Like me, you have probably mustered up costumes of grandeur on their behalf, even begging the people at Party City to scour the backroom for the perfect piece for your princess. You paid way more money for it than you planned to spend, but the smile on her face made it worthwhile. She was a shining beacon on stage. You recorded it and excessively shared pictures online because you are that parent. We all are.

The tedious part comes into play because out of the longest 60 minutes of your life, your precious shines only for 2.3 seconds. Every other proud mom, dad, grandma, and grandpa has their own star to make over, so you sit and wait during their moments, trying not to look as though you're planning dinner for the next month, making your grocery list on your smartphone.

You Can't Fight a Battle When You're Thirsty

This was me a few months ago. During our spring school perfor-mance, I was marking time in my seat, praying the minutes might supernaturally tick by a bit faster than God ordains them. Having applauded my own kindergarten pilgrim girl, I was ready to be acting on my now-made grocery list when one of the other classes began a short play about a woman turned folk legend from the Revolutionary War. Her name was Molly Pitcher. At least that's what they all started calling a woman named Mary who was the wife of a barber turned soldier for the Continental Army. During the Battle of Monmouth in Freehold, New Jersey, on June 28, 1778, she made repeated trips to the nearby watering hole to fill pitchers of water for the soldiers. She walked tirelessly around the battlefield offering cold drinks to battle-weary men. Legend also tells us when her husband was injured dur-ing the battle, she took over his cannon duties. Molly Pitcher was also a gunner. She got the job done.

Obviously, I looked up from planning my grocery list during this portion of the school presentation. It was almost as if God had tapped me on the shoulder to make sure I was paying close attention as a sweet third grader in continental dress delivered her one line: "You can't fight a battle if you are thirsty." I was stunned. Right there in the middle of the third- and fourth-grade Revolutionary War tribute God spoke to me. His own words echoed in my heart from a previous study of his Word:

> Jesus said to her, "Everyone who drinks of this water will be thirsty again, but whoever drinks of the water that I will give him will never be thirsty again. The water that I will give him will become in him a spring of water welling up to eternal life" (John 4:13-14).

This truth was powerfully joined to another verse, reminding me of the power of God's Word.

> Husbands, you must love your wives so deeply, purely, and sacrificially that we can understand it only when we com-pare it to the love the Anointed One has for His bride, the

church. We know He gave Himself up completely to make her His own, washing her clean of all her impurity with water and the powerful presence of His word (Ephesians 5:25-26 THE VOICE).

God's Word quenches the spiritual thirst in our hearts. It washes us clean and shows us his radical love for his bride, the church. I think the writer of Hebrews was looking at a battle-weary group of believers and wanted to hold out a water-filled weapon they needed in their arsenal. They could not fight the battle thirsty. They needed to drink deep from the well. He wanted them to know God's Word does something to us, in us, and through us. But first they would have to pay attention to it.

If I've Told You Once, I've Told You Five Times

When something is important, you repeat it. In my house you'll hear me say over and over again, "Stop running." "Put your dishes in the sink." "Turn down the volume on the television." And my personal favorite, "Walk the dog." These aren't hard things to remember, but for some reason my girls have selective memory. Of course, we have repeated conversations about spiritual truths as well. My girls know without a doubt that we are going to talk about God's Word and pray a little or a lot each day. Although we do have times of purposeful study, we tend to talk about things along the way in the spirit of Deuteronomy 6.

Mostly, we talk while I'm driving them to all the places they need to be. Because after all these years of mothering I have come to realize what I truly am is a professional driver. I'm also a snack giver. It would seem as well that my best moments are while driving and dispensing snacks. I mean, this is multitasking at its best when you can navigate traffic and dig in your oversized purse for fish-shaped cheddar crackers. During these winning moments of mothering, my girls might cringe when I accidentally (or rather purposely) repeat a story with spiritual significance, starting with the phrase "When I was younger." They have no qualms about telling me they've heard it before, many times. You should know, I have no qualms in ignoring them and telling them anyway.

The writer of Hebrews didn't tell his readers once to pay attention to the Word and the One speaking it; he mentioned it over and over again.

- Hebrews 2:1: "Therefore we must pay much closer attention to what we have heard, lest we drift away from it." (They have heard the Word spoken already.)

- Hebrews 3:1: "Consider Jesus, the apostle…of our confession." (Apostle = the one who speaks the Word.)

- Hebrews 3:12: "Take care, brothers, lest there be in any of you an evil, unbelieving heart." (A heart not hearing and believing the Word.)

- Hebrews 3:15: "Today, if you hear his voice, do not harden your hearts." (His voice = the Word.)

- Hebrews 4:2: "Good news came to us just as to them, but the message they heard did not benefit them, because they were not united by faith with those who listened." (The Word benefits us when combined with faith.)

Building throughout the first few chapters, he was bringing to light the centrality of the Word of God in the life of every believer. They needed this repetition because, apparently, they had selective memory, much like my daughters. They might have rolled their eyes a time or two, because what was at stake for them was their maturity. The writer also felt it was necessary to bring up the topic once again in chapter 5 and chapter 6. I think he must have had a bee in his bonnet about the matter. I love what Warren Wiersbe says about this.

> Our relationship to the Word of God determines our spiritual maturity. The people had drifted from the Word (2:1-3), doubted the Word (Chaps 3-4), and become dull toward the Word. They had not mixed the Word with faith (4:2) and practiced it in their daily lives (5:14)…instead of going forward (6:1) they were going backward.[1]

Maturity and moving forward sound similar to what we talked

about in the last chapter about Abraham. You have already seen what happened in his life when he drifted from the word God spoke to him and he doubted. When he mixed the word of God with faith, he moved forward and spiritual maturity was on glorious display in his life.

I would like to skip the parts of my story when I've drifted, doubted, and grown dull to the Word of God. I want to heed the warnings and exhortations of the writer of Hebrews once and for all. I want to be found paying attention, considering, and exchanging my unbelieving heart for a faith that endures. God has not left us on our own. To help us in our own unbelief we have the living Word of God. Gratefully, in Hebrews 4:12 we have one of the most visually stunning verses in the Bible. It tells us what the Word of God is and what it does.

> The word of God is living and active, sharper than any two-edged sword, piercing to the division of soul and of spirit, of joints and of marrow, and discerning the thoughts and intentions of the heart.

The Word of God Is…

Living

You may know I have an almost nerd-like affection for the study of words. I get downright giddy over dictionaries. Don't get me started on my crush on Webster's 1828 dictionary. I hope you can put up with me for a moment as we dig a little deeper into the individual words that make up this verse. I know we can get bogged down in many details, but if you humor me for a moment or two, I think this verse will forever be engrained in your mind as it is for me.

The word *word*, or *logos* in the Greek, means "a word, uttered by a living voice, embodies a concept or idea, what someone has said, the sayings of God."[2] If you want to completely geek out with me, you will love to know *logos* was first used by a Greek philosopher named Heraclitus around 600 BC to designate the divine reason or plan that coordinates a changing universe. The Greeks, you see, didn't have any trouble believing their gods, and our God spoke with real words. Words could be divinely wrought and they often were.

The word *living*, or *quick* as some Bible translations use, is the Greek word *zaō*. It means "to live, breathe, be among the living (not lifeless, not dead), to have true life and be worthy of the name, active, blessed, endless in the kingdom of God."[3]

> When we come to the Word of God we need to know it is not like any other book. It is breathing, endless, and has true life apart from us.

The writer was basically saying, by putting *logos* and *zaō* together, "the living word is living." Was he repeating himself on purpose? Perhaps he was. Maybe he was simply blessed to have the repertoire of Greek language at his disposal. Should we have any doubt what he is saying is truth? When we come to the Word of God we need to know it is not like any other book. It is breathing, endless, and has true life apart from us. I like what R.C. Sproul once said about this.

> When I was hired to teach the Scriptures in required Bible courses at a Christian college, the president of the institution phoned me and said, "We need someone young and exciting, someone with a dynamic method who will be able to 'make the Bible come alive.'" I had to force myself to swallow my words. I wanted to say, "You want me to make the Bible come alive? I didn't know that it had died. In fact, I never even heard that it was ill. Who was the attending physician at the Bible's demise?" No, I can't make the Bible come alive for anyone. The Bible is already alive. It makes me come alive.[4]

> It is not your job to make the Word of God come alive. The living Word of God is living.

My friend, let the tremendous grace of the living Word fall fresh on you right here. Of everything you have to do today, it is not your job to make the Word of God come alive. You may have to wash dishes, tackle the laundry pile, and make a trip to the grocery store. Maybe you need to do those things again tomorrow. But you don't have to sit in front of God's Word and hope it comes alive. The living Word of God is living. Believe it and let it bring life to your weary heart.

Active (Powerful)

Sometimes the Greek word gives us a quick clue as to what it means in English. The word used here is *energēs*. Have you ever considered God's Word as possessing powerful energy? God's Word is not still. It has magnificent power. This reminds me of the first chapter of Genesis when God spoke the world into being. Just as his word empowered and brought the world into existence, it is moving powerfully in our lives as well. The Voice translation of the first part of Hebrews 4:12 says, "The word of God, you see, is alive and moving." A note under the verse adds by way of commentary, "By God's word, everything finds a rhythm, a place. It fills, empowers, enlivens, and redeems us." God's Word breathed out gives cadence to our lives and sets them firmly in place. His Word moves us powerfully toward redemption. Can your heart take more? Well, hold on, my friend, because of course it just keeps getting better.

Sharper (Than Any Two-Edged Sword)

The beauty and selection of the word used by the writer becomes crystal clear when you compare it to another word he could have chosen. *Tomos* (used here) means "sharper," as if able to cut by a single stroke.[5] *Koptō* also means to cut, but this type of cutting is more akin to our word *hack* or *chop*.[6] *Tomos* is more decisive. It means a single swift stroke is all that's needed to cut to the quick. God's Word does not need repeated blows as a single-edged sword might require.

> It is effective and efficient.
> It is sharper than any two-edged sword.

It cuts both ways.
It is the sword of the Spirit (Ephesians 6:17).
It is the two-edged sword that comes out of
     the mouth of Christ (Revelation 1:16).
It is sharper than any two-edged sword, *for it will enter
where no sword can and make a more critical dissection:* It
pierces to the dividing asunder of the soul and the spirit
(emphasis mine).[7]

God's living, moving Word goes where no other weapon can—
straight to the most critical point with surgical precision. What does it
do once it is there in this secret place of our hearts?

> This is no fluffy interchange between my heart and God's
> Word. If I have any sin secretly hidden where my soul
> and spirit meet, you can believe God's Word will find it.

The Word of God Does

The living, active Word of God does something to us and within us.
First, with quick and decisive work, it exposes us and "strikes through
to the place where soul and spirit meet, to the innermost intimacies
of a man's being: It exposes the very thoughts and motives of man's
heart" (Hebrews 4:12 PHILLIPS). This is no fluffy interchange between
my heart and God's Word. If I have any sin secretly hidden where my
soul and spirit meet, you can believe God's Word will find it. When I
believe a paralyzing lie from the Enemy, God's Word will cut it down
meticulously. His sword divides and destroys anything in disagreement
with truth. And just to make sure we are clear on the matter, the writer
goes on to state unapologetically, "No creature can hide from God;
God sees all. Everyone and everything is exposed, open for His inspec-
tion; and He's the One we will have to explain ourselves to" (Hebrews
4:13 THE VOICE).

> Unveiled and laid bare by God's Word, I'm an
> open book. It reads me as much as I read it.

I've become pretty skilled over the years at hiding from people all around me. I have at times fooled them for weeks and years on end that I have it all together. I have even let pride enter my life and find a home in my heart, thinking I could do everything in my own strength. But the minute I choose to give God's Word the access it so desperately seeks to my heart, everything is exposed. Unveiled and laid bare by God's Word, I'm an open book. It reads me as much as I read it.

> Thankfully, what God exposes and
> inspects, he resurrects and revives.

Remember I said God's Word does something *to* us? It also does something *in* us. Thankfully, what God exposes and inspects, he resurrects and revives. His desire is to cure my unbelief and keep me (and you) from sinning. He doesn't make quick work of our hearts merely to wound us. His intention is to heal us and lead us to his mercy:

> Since then we have a Great High Priest who has passed through the heavens, Jesus, the Son of God, let us hold fast our confession. For we do not have a high priest who is unable to sympathize with our weaknesses, but one who in every respect has been tempted as we are, yet without sin. Let us then with confidence draw near to the throne of grace, that we may receive mercy and find grace to help in time of need (Hebrews 4:14-16).

Take heart, sister. God does not leave us unveiled and laid bare for long. Most importantly, he does not leave us alone. We have this wonderful provision, the same one who offered living water to the woman spiritually dying of thirst by the side of a fountain, acting as our Great High Priest and mediator. He himself sits on the throne we are bid to come to and drink deeply from. And what our hearts need most, he pours out endlessly. As I wrote in my book *Fresh Out of Amazing*…

> The invitation here is simply to come to the throne of grace and receive what we need. Of course, it's hard to receive anything before you are fresh out of amazing. If you don't have a need, you won't come. But when you are emptied, when you're aware of all the places you're lacking, when you're weak and weary, you can more easily give yourself permission to come. And you need to come.
>
> Aligning my life with this truth looks like the act of coming to God's throne and receiving his grace. I need to plant myself front and center at the throne of grace and gaze upon Jesus. It is a habit I am slowly learning. I'm so grateful he is a gentle and patient teacher.[8]

Time and time again when I have been weak and weary, God has used his Word to heal my heart. This was true that day years ago when I showed up to study the book of Hebrews for the first time. Not one time in my life have I come seeking to be filled up only to be denied by God. I think this is why I can't stop telling women about my love for God's Word.

If you ever hear me speak or read anything else I've written, you'll probably come to a part much like this chapter, where I sound a bit like a broken record. It just matters that much. I will always do my best to leave you with the encouragement to be a woman who sits at the feet of Jesus and receives his mercy through engaging with his powerful Word. I can't stop, and I won't stop. I spent years treating God's Word as an accessory I carried to church or pulled out to write a Bible verse on a note for a friend. Until I hit rock bottom and God used it to put the pieces of my heart back together I did not realize his Word is so much more than a crutch. It's a sword. I wanted to be a woman who knew how to use it once and for all. I think you, since we are now officially girlfriends, will not be surprised I want the same for you.

As If Your Life Depended on It

I met my friend Robin in 1989 at Indiana University when I crashed her Bible study. I guess showing up to a Bible study unannounced is not really the same thing as coming to a party without an invitation. Still, it was probably one of the boldest things I have ever done. They had been meeting for weeks when I arrived with Mary, a girl I barely knew who lived on my dormitory floor. I was lost on that Big Ten campus in a sea of people. I knew in my heart I needed to find a group of girlfriends who loved Jesus—and fast.

I remember that first night as if it were yesterday. I was gripping my black paperback NIV Student Bible as though it were a shield, afraid these girls might think I was small and uninteresting. Instead they opened their circle and ultimately their hearts wide as we bonded over our new life as college students and dived deep into the pages of God's Word. That one brave step changed the course of my life forever.

Last week, Robin arrived a few miles from my front door on vacation. I drove over to the beach condo she was staying in, and we parked our two chairs right in front of the water and watched as her boys dived in and out of the surf and two of my girls played in the sand as mermaids. We quickly talked about life and friends, and then we landed on the one subject that has bonded our lives since that first day in 1989—God's Word. It sure makes my heart smile to know that when I crashed her Bible study, God knew we'd still be talking about his Word three decades later. He planned it that way and I'm so humbled by that. As we shared what God has been teaching us, Robin reminded me of a passage from Deuteronomy:

> When Moses had finished speaking all these words to all Israel, he said to them, "Take to heart all the words by which I am warning you today, that you may command them to your children, that they may be careful to do all the words of this law. For it is no empty word for you, but your very life, and by this word you shall live long in the land that you are going over the Jordan to possess" (32:45-47).

The last words of Moses pertained to the Word of God. He was telling Israel they needed to be careful to do all that God had said as though their lives depended on it. God's Word held life and blessing. It is the same for us today. His Word has not ceased being life-giving. We can come to it every day as though *our* lives depend on it, because they do.

As I've thought long and prayed hard, I've decided it would be a good idea for me to give you a tool for studying the Word on your own. Now, let me say many great tools are out there for Bible study. This is not the only tool available. But, as a girlfriend, I think I would be remiss for not handing you something you could use to help you grow in your walk with God and love for his Word. This is something you can use in your personal Bible study or with friends.

LIFE Bible Study Method

L—Listen to God's Word

I—Investigate

F—Face-to-Face

E—Experience in Real Life

L—Listen to God's Word

When we come to a passage from the Bible—a verse, a chapter, or an entire book—we need to listen to the words. My advice is to read the passage several times. I like to read it in different translations as well. There is no time frame for this. Just read and enjoy the words.

In addition to reading the words, I like to write them. You can do this a number of different ways. When I write through a passage I use a loose form of diagramming. Mind you, I don't pull out my grammar books and make sure it's perfect. I simply diagram it in a way that helps the heart of the verse or passage pop out.

Another way of writing it is to put it into your own words. A Bible teacher told me one time that if you can say it in your own words, it will stick better. Feel free to put your written words in a fun, hard-copy journal or, like me, you might prefer to put them in a note-taking program on your computer. The bottom line for me is that reading Scripture several times and then writing it helps me to listen better and hear what God is saying to my heart. It's a perfect first step.

I—Investigate

Once you've spent some time familiarizing yourself with the passage you're studying, it's time to dig into the text. If listening is akin to stepping back and looking at the bigger picture, investigating involves zooming in and looking for details and connections. A simple study Bible and dictionary—and if you are tech savvy, an internet connection—are really all you need. I also pay special attention during the investigation phase to key words. A key word is a word in the text that is either important or repeated. Maybe as you read through the text you notice a theme or word used again and again. My advice to you is to chase down that word. Look it up in the dictionary and make sure you know what it means. If you are like me, you may want to uncover the writer's meaning with a basic Hebrew (Old Testament) or Greek (New Testament) word study based on which book of the Bible you're studying.

Because context is important, you'll want to also know what comes before and after the passage as well as what kind of writing it is. Many study Bibles' individual book introductions are filled with great background information. It is perfectly fine to start there and build out on your own.

You might also use this time to look for other verses in Scripture that form a connection with this passage. This is called a cross-reference. Most basic study Bibles will list these at the bottom of the page. Because the best interpreter of a passage of Scripture is another passage from Scripture, it's good to make note of these at this time. Just list them, look them up, and note anything that helps you understand or supports your current passage.

You can spend as much time here as you like. You better believe I love a good word chase and digging for connections. I think this is where so many lightbulb moments happen for me. You know, when you get so excited you say, "Wow, I had no idea!" God continually encourages my heart as I look at the depth of meaning in his Word.

> When we open God's Word we come
> face-to-face with him.

F—Face-to-Face

Remember how when Isaiah came face-to-face with God his response was to fall on his face and worship? Friends, when we open God's Word we come face-to-face with him. My pastor, David Uth, tells us the Bible is the only book you read where the author actually shows up. When we dive deep into his Holy Word, he meets us on the page and in our hearts. More than a few times tears have come to my eyes as I've been studying. I am moved by what I'm reading.

> Worship from the deepest parts of your soul. Sing. Write it down. Sit with silent adorations. Tell him, friends. Tell him.

Sometimes—many times—I'm convicted of sin in my life and I know I need to stop right then and tell God I'm sorry for it. Other times I want to raise my hands to praise him for the specific and swift encouragement he has just laid on my heart. He is just so good to us. I can't imagine creating a Bible study method that didn't encourage you to come to your Savior with gratitude, worship, and prayerful conversations. This is our time to tell him what is in our hearts. Tell him. Worship from the deepest parts of your soul. Sing. Write it down. Sit with silent adorations. Tell him, friends. Tell him.

E—Experience in Real Life

As we read and study God's Word, it changes and matures us. It is absolutely awesome if you have a plan to study God's Word. It is better for you to be moved to worship as you do. But if the truth you encounter there doesn't make an impact on your everyday life and make you more like Jesus, you have missed a large portion of the point. Make a commitment to allow the living and active Word of God to do what it was designed to do.

Personally, living out God's Word in real life means I need to dwell on the words I'm reading. I may try to memorize a verse or two to let the passage I've been studying stick with me for a while. It always helps me to talk about it with another person, and of course, to write about it.

> The living Word of God is moving; we
> need to follow where it leads.

After I've saturated my heart with the passage, I need to take note of what action is needed. Now, the action is not always big and bold. Sometimes it's simply using kinder words with my girls or looking for opportunities to serve others as I go about my day. Other times God gets all up in my business and calls me out to speak a word to others I wouldn't dream of saying on my own. It varies. But in the depth of my heart, I know when God is moving me to take action on a truth he has revealed. The living Word of God is moving; we need to follow where it leads.

A Final Word on the Word

I'm sitting in my local office, Panera, wishing you were sitting across from me so I could make firm eye contact with you. I'd love to know if you are tracking with me or wishing I would just quit meddling. If my words fall short, don't miss this impassioned plea from an old man who took a million or so slaves out of Egypt and brought them through a 40-year walk in the wilderness: "For it is no empty word for you, but your very life" (Deuteronomy 32:47).

The Word is your very life, sweet girl. And whether you move forward or fall back, your maturity in Christ depends on it. The Word is also a love letter for your heart on the hard days when you would rather quit. It will be the sword in your hand when you need to fight. Quite simply, it's the voice of the one who was willing to become like you so you could become like him. He is the one who sits on the throne but left the glory of heaven to save you.

> God made very sure that we could understand who he
> is, what he is like, and what he wants for us and what he

wants from us. He did this by sending his Son, Jesus. Now we don't have just the written Word, we have the Living Word—a real person. When people watched Jesus, they were seeing God.[9]

It is a living Word. His name is Jesus. He is speaking. Are you listening?

LIFE Bible Study
Method at a Glance

L—Listen to God's Word

- Read the passage multiple times.
- Read it in different Bible translations.
- Enjoy the Word.
- Write it out—diagram it.
- Write it in your own words.

I—Investigate

- Dig into the text.
- Look for details and connections.
- Look up key words.
- Notice context (what comes before and after).
- Cross-reference other key Scripture.

F—Face-to-Face

- Remember that God meets you on the page and in your heart.

- Worship from the deepest parts of your soul. Sing. Write down your response. Sit with silent adoration. Pray.

E—Experience in Real Life

- Allow the living and active Word to transform you.

- Dwell in it.

- Memorize it.

- Take note of what change is needed.

- Live it out.

Notes

Chapter 1

1. Louie Giglio, *Goliath Must Fall: Winning the Battle Against Your Giants* (Nashville, TN: Thomas Nelson Publishers, 2017), 81.

2. Stacey Thacker, *Hope for the Weary Mom Devotional* (Eugene, OR, Harvest House Publishers, 2015), 36.

3. A.W. Tozer, *The Root of the Righteous* (Chicago: Moody Publishers, 2015), 11–12.

4. Milton Vincent, *A Gospel Primer for Christians: Learning to See the Glories of God's Love* (Bemidji, MN: Focus Publishing, 2008), 13.

5. The Voice Bible, note on Ephesians 1 (The Voice Bible, copyright © 2012 Thomas Nelson, Inc. The Voice™ translation © 2012 Ecclesia Bible Society. All rights reserved).

6. Elisabeth Elliot, "The Search for Significance," Blueletterbible.com, audio accessed April 26, 2017.

7. Stacey Thacker, *Is Jesus Worth It?* (Eugene, OR, Harvest House Publishers, 2017), 38.

8. S.V. "Sealed," blueletterbible.org.

9. Tony Merida, *Christ-Centered Exposition Commentary: Exalting Jesus in Ephesians* (Nashville, TN: B&H Publishers, 2014), 31.

10. Alexander Maclaren, PreceptsAustin.com, http://www.preceptaustin.org/ephesians_13-4#am%201:3, accessed May 5, 2017.

Chapter 2

1. Merida, *Christ-Centered Exposition*, 4.

2. Warren Wiersbe, *Be Bible Study Series*, Bible Gateway.com, https://www.biblegateway.com/passage/?search=john%208&version=ESV, accessed July 5, 2017.

3. Merida, *Christ-Centered Exposition*, 6.

4. Cornelius R. Stam, "Paul, The Apostle of Grace," https://www.bereanbiblesociety.org/paul-the-apostle-of-grace/, accessed July 12, 2017.

5. Merida, *Christ-Centered Exposition*, 45.

6. Merida, *Christ-Centered Exposition*, 46.

7. Tony Rienke, *Newton on the Christian Life: To Live Is Christ* (Wheaton, IL: Crossway Publishers, 2015), 22.

8. Rienke, *Newton on the Christian Life*, 47–48.

9. You can listen to Britt's full story on the Chatologie podcast with Angie Elkins at http://www .chatologie.com/episode-10-britt-nelson/.

10. Vincent, *A Gospel Primer for Christians*, 32.

Chapter 3

1. Lysa TerKeurst, *Uninvited* (Nashville, TN: Thomas Nelson, 2016), 18.

2. Sally Lloyd-Jones, *The Jesus Storybook Bible* (Grand Rapids, MI: Zondervan, 2007), 17.

3. Brennan Manning, *Abba's Child* (Colorado Springs, CO: NavPress, 2002), 55.

4. Chuck Swindoll, PreceptsAustin.org, http://salemnet.vo.llnwd.net/o29/insightforliving/images/ ifl-usa/content/ascendio/resources/bible/49-Ephesians.png, accessed July 26, 2017.

5. Warren Wiersbe, *Be Rich: Gaining Things That Money Can't Buy* (Colorado Springs, CO: David C Cook, 2009), 69.

6. Matthew Henry, Bible Gateway, https://www.biblegateway.com/passage/?search=Ephesians%20 2%3A11-21&version=ESV, accessed July 31, 2017.

7. S.V., "reconcile," Webster's Dictionary of 1828, http://webstersdictionary1828.com/Dictionary/ reconcile.

8. Merida, *Christ-Centered Exposition,* 67.

9. "Florida Beachgoers Form Human Chain to Save Family," https://www.usatoday.com/story/ news/nation-now/2017/07/11/florida-beachgoers-form-human-chain/467152001/, July 11, 2017.

10. "Florida Beachgoers Form Human Chain to Save Family."

Chapter 4

1. Vincent, *A Gospel Primer for Christians*, 36.

2. Angela Lee Duckworth, TED.com, "Grit: The Power of Passion and Perseverance," https:// www.ted.com/talks/angela_lee_duckworth_grit_the_power_of_passion_and_perseverance/ transcript, April 2013.

3. Duckworth, TED.com, "Grit: The Power of Passion and Perseverance."

4. Andrew Murray, *With Christ in the School of Prayer* (New Kensington, PA: Whitaker House, 1981), 7.

5. James E. Rosscup, "The Importance of Prayer in Ephesians," *The Master's Seminary Journal* 6, no.1 (Spring 1995), 58.

6. Matthew Henry, Biblegateway.com, https://www.biblegateway.com/passage/?search=Ephesian s+1&version=ESV, accessed August 28, 2017.

7. Wiersbe, *Be Rich,* 45.

8. S.V. "power," Blueletterbible.org, https://www.blueletterbible.org/lang/lexicon/lexicon.cfm? Strongs=G1411&t=KJV, accessed 02/10/2018.

9. Merida, *Christ-Centered Exposition*, 82.

10. Merida, *Christ-Centered Exposition*, 84.

11. S.V., "comprehend," blueletterbible.com.org, https://www.blueletterbible.org/lang/lexicon/lex-icon.cfm?Strongs=G2638&t=KJV, accessed September 2, 2017.

12. S.V., "fullness," blueletterbible.org, https://www.blueletterbible.org/lang/lexicon/lexicon.cfm ?Strongs=G4138&t=KJV, accessed June 5, 2017.

13. Matthew Henry, Bible Gateway, https://www.biblegateway.com/passage/?search=Ephesians%20 3%3A20-21&version=ESV, accessed July 31, 2017.

14. Murray, *With Christ in the School of Prayer*, 25.

15. Murray, *With Christ in the School of Prayer*, 10.

Chapter 5

1. Watchman Nee, *Sit, Walk, Stand* (Carol Stream, IL: Tyndale House Publishers, 1977), 22–23.

2. *The Women's Evangelical Commentary of the New Testament*, "Worth" (Nashville, TN: B&H Publishing, 2011), 550.

3. S.V. "humility," bluelettebible.org, https://www.blueletterbible.org/lang/lexicon/lexicon.cfm ?Strongs=G5012&t=KJV, accessed September 13, 2017.

4. *The Women's Evangelical Commentary of the New Testament*, 551.

5. Brooke McGlothlin, *Gospel-Centered Mom* (Colorado Spring, CO: Multnomah Publishers, 2017), 38–39.

6. *The Women's Evangelical Commentary of the New Testament*, 549.

7. Merida, *Christ-Centered Exposition*, 118.

Chapter 6

1. Priscilla Shirer, *The Armor of God* (Nashville, TN: Lifeway, 2015), 5.

2. S.V. "Be Strong," blueletterbible.org, (https://www.blueletterbible.org/lang/lexicon/lexicon .cfm?Strongs=G1743&t=KJV), accessed September 25, 2017.

3. Merida, *Christ-Centered Exposition*, 176.

4. Lisa Whittle, *Put Your Warrior Boots On* (Eugene, OR: Harvest House Publishers, 2017)

5. Merida, *Christ-Centered Exposition*, 174.

6. Lindsey Cheney, The Pleated Poppy, http://thepleatedpoppy.com.

7. S.V. "devil," blueletterbible.org, https://www.blueletterbible.org/lang/lexicon/lexicon.cfm ?Strongs=G1228&t=KJV, accessed September 26, 2017.

8. Shirer, *The Armor of God*, 11.

9. Merida, *Christ-Centered Exposition*, 177.

10. Nee, *Sit, Walk, Stand*, 42.

11. Shirer, *The Armor of God*, 52.

12. Erin Warren, via-email newsletter, firstorlando.com, http://us13.campaign-archive? com/?u=ea dcfb49bacafa8ab60763rd88&id=c101964ccc&e=ce/c3bee99, January 17, 2017.

13. S.V. "peace," Blueletterbible.org, https://www.blueletterbible.org/lang/lexicon/lexicon.cfm? Strongs=G1515&t=KJV, accessed September 30, 2017.

14. S.V. "faith," Blueletterbible.org, https://www.blueletterbible.org/lang/lexicon/lexicon.cfm?pag e=3&strongs=G4102&t=KJV#lexResults, assessed September 30, 2017.

15. Chip Ingram, *The Invisible War* (Ada, MI: Baker Books, 2008), 134.

Chapter 7

1. John Eagen, as quoted in Brennan Manning, *Abba's Child* (Colorado Springs, CO: NavPress, 2002), 51.

2. S.V. "love," Blueletterbible.org, https://www.blueletterbible.org/lang/lexicon/lexicon.cfm?Strongs =G25&t=KJV, accessed October 2, 2017.

3. Manning, *Abba's Child*, 52.

4. Matthew Henry, *The Whole Commentary of the Bible*, Bible Gateway.com, https://www.bible gateway.com/passage/?search=2+Corinthians+2%3A14-17&version=ESV, accessed October 14, 2017.

5. Manning, *Abba's Child*, 60.

6. Frederick M. Lehman, "The Love of God," http://library.timelesstruths.org/music/The_Love_ of_God/, accessed October 14, 2017.

The Word

1. Warren Wiersbe, *Wiersbe's Expository Outlines on the New Testament* (Colorado Springs, CO: David C Cook, 1992), 690.

2. S.V. Word: Blueletterbible.org, https://www.blueletterbible.org/lang/lexicon/lexicon.cfm ?Strongs =G3056&t=KJV, accessed 06/23/16.

3. S.V. Living: Blueletterbible.org, https://www.blueletterbible.org/lang/lexicon/lexicon.cfm ?Strongs =G2198&t=KJV, accessed 06/23/16.

4. R.C. Sproul, *Knowing Scripture* (Downers Grove: IL: InterVarsity Press, 1977), 14–15.

5. S.V. Tomos: Blueletterbible.org, https://www.blueletterbible.org/lang/lexicon/lexicon.cfm ?Strongs =G5114&t=KJVm accessed 06/24/16.

6. S.V. Koptō: blueletterbible.org, https://www.blueletterbible.org/lang/lexicon/lexicon.cfm ?trongs =G2875&t=KJV, accessed 06/24/16.

7. Matthew Henry, *Matthew Henry Commentary on the Whole Bible* (Complete), https://www.bible gateway.com/passage/?search=hebrews%204%3A12&version=ESV, accessed 06/24/16.

8. Stacey Thacker, *Fresh Out of Amazing* (Eugene, OR: Harvest House Publishers, 2016), 177–78.

9. John Piper, DesiringGod.org, http://www.desiringgod.org/articles/lenten-lights, 03/24/16.

Acknowledgments

I've learned over the past few years that books don't write themselves and a writer certainly doesn't write alone in a cabin in the woods. It takes a village, and these are the best kind of people who make my village work and help my words fly. Thank you seems so small, but here goes:

Mike: I'm thanking Jesus every day for his kindness to us and getting another chance to do this life with you. I'm grateful for your encouragement and support of my love of writing and words. I could not do this without you. I love you, always.

Emma, Abigail, Caroline, and Alison: I could not be prouder to be your mom. Watching each of you walk with Jesus, this year especially, has been a gift. Thanks for letting me write every summer for the past four years. You are so loved!

IU Cru Girl (Lisa, Robin, Stephanie, Tricia, Judy, Samantha, and Unchong): You are my people. Two thousand seventeen was a year none of us would have chosen, but I'm grateful we walk together in grace with Christ.

Erin Warren: Thank you for helping me grow closer to Jesus in this hardest year and for always bringing me coffee. Your enthusiasm for Girlfriend Groups has been life-giving! I love you, dear friend!

Angie Elkins: I will always come to your house for Bible study and cohosting your Chatologie podcast. Your support of this book has made such a difference in my ability to write it. Love you so!

Britt Nelson: Thank you for bravely sharing your story with Emma first and letting it settle in deep here on the page for all of us girlfriends. I love how grace walked into your life!

Tanya Cramer: Thank you for constantly supporting my words and reminding me that sometimes God doesn't want us to see through it—but he is always present in it! Love you, friend!

Kathleen Kerr: Thank you for how you make my words sing in the most beautiful way. Let's keep going.

Harvest House Team: Thank you for allowing me to pen words and put them in the hands of women all over the world.

Janet Grant: I love how God has woven this series together. You saw it first, and I am beyond grateful for your wisdom and experience. Thank you so much!

Jesus: I love you. First. Always. Forever.

About the Author

Stacey Thacker is a wife and the mother of four girls. The author of five books, she is also a Bible teacher with a passion to connect with women and encourage them in their walks with God. You can find her blogging at staceythacker.com and hanging out on Instagram and Twitter @staccythacker, usually with a cup of coffee in her hand.

Also by Stacey Thacker

Hope for the Weary Mom

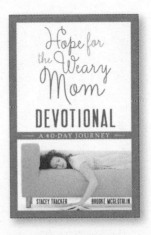

Hope for the Weary
Mom Devotional:
A 40-Day Journey

Fresh Out of Amazing

Is Jesus Worth It?
(Girlfriends' Guide to the
Bible Book 1—Hebrews)

To learn more about Harvest House books and
to read sample chapters, visit our website:

www.harvesthousepublishers.com

HARVEST HOUSE PUBLISHERS
EUGENE, OREGON